IELTS Speaking Test Practice Book with IELTS Speaking Topics, Strategies, and 300 Practice Test Questions for the Academic and General Modules

IELTS is jointly owned by the British Council, IDP: IELTS Australia, and Cambridge English Language Assessments, which are neither affiliated with nor endorse this publication.

IELTS Speaking Test Practice Book with IELTS Speaking Topics, Strategies, and 300 Practice Test Questions for the Academic and General Modules

© COPYRIGHT 1995, 2014, 2021. IELTS Success Associates dba www.examsam.com

All rights reserved. No part of this publication may be reproduced, stored in a retrieval system, or transmitted, in any form or by any means, electronic, mechanical, photocopying, recording or otherwise.

ISBN: 978-1-949282-80-1

COPYRIGHT NOTICE TO EDUCATORS: Please respect copyright law. Under no circumstances may you make copies of these materials for distribution to or use by students. Should you wish to use the materials with students, you are required to purchase a copy of this publication for each of your students.

NOTE: IELTS is jointly owned by the British Council, IDP: IELTS Australia, and Cambridge English Language Assessments, which are neither affiliated with nor endorse this publication.

TABLE OF CONTENTS

PART 1 – IELTS Speaking Test Overview

    IELTS Speaking Test Format   1

    Parts of the IELTS Speaking Test   2

    How the IELTS Speaking Test Is Scored   3

    How to Prepare for the IELTS Speaking Test   5

    Tips for Better Performance on Your IELTS Speaking Test   7

PART 2 – Grammar and Verb Tense on Each Task of the Speaking Test   10

PART 3 – Conditional Sentence Review

    Using Conditional Sentences to Improve Your Speaking Test Score   12

    The Zero Conditional   13

    Zero Conditional – Exercises   14

    Zero Conditional – Answers to the Exercises   15

    The First Conditional   16

    Comparing the Zero and First Conditionals   17

    First Conditional – Exercises   18

    First Conditional – Answers to the Exercises   19

    The Second Conditional   20

    Comparing the First and Second Conditionals   22

    Second Conditional – Exercises   23

    Second Conditional – Answers to the Exercises   24

    The Third Conditional   25

    Third Conditional – Exercises   26

    Third Conditional – Answers to the Exercises   27

    Deciding Which Conditional to Use – Exercises   28

    Deciding Which Conditional to Use – Answers and Explanations   30

PART 4 – Overview of the Three Individual Tasks

IELTS Speaking Exam – Task 1:

    Overview of Speaking Task 1   32

    How to Prepare for Speaking Task 1   34

    Speaking Task 1 – Sample Response and Exercise   35

    Speaking Task 1 – Answer to the Exercise   37

IELTS Speaking Exam – Task 2:

    Overview of Speaking Task 2   39

    How to Prepare for Speaking Task 2   40

    Speaking Task 2 – Sample Response and Exercise   42

    Speaking Task 2 – Answer to the Exercise   44

IELTS Speaking Exam – Task 3:

    Overview of Speaking Task 3   46

    How to Prepare for Speaking Task 3   47

    Speaking Task 3 – Sample Response and Exercise   48

    Speaking Task 3 – Answer to the Exercise   51

PART 5 – Useful Phrases for the Speaking Test

    Talking about the Present   54

    Talking about the Past   54

    Collecting Your Thoughts   55

    Emphasising   55

    Explaining What You Mean   55

    Giving Examples   56

    Giving Your Opinion   56

Giving Others' Opinions	57
Giving Generalisations	57
Comparing and Contrasting	57
Describing and Explaining	58
Giving Advice	58
Speculating and Predicting	59

PART 6 – Vocabulary Usage on the Speaking Test

Culture and Society	61
Education	61
Environment	62
Family, Friends and Colleagues	63
Food and Nutrition	64
Free Time, Hobbies and Leisure	64
Historical Buildings	65
Housing	66
Newspapers, Media and Technology	67
People	68
Places	69
Relationships	70
Shopping	70
Social Problems	71
Television	72
Transport	73
Travel and Tourism	74

PART 7 – 3 Practice Speaking Tests with Model Answers

Practice Speaking Test 1:

    Task 1   75

    Task 2   76

    Task 3   77

Models Answers to Practice Speaking Test 1:

    Model Answer to Task 1   78

    Comments on Model Answer to Task 1   80

    Model Answer to Task 2   82

    Comments on Model Answer to Task 2   84

    Model Answer to Task 3   86

    Comments on Model Answer to Task 3   89

Practice Speaking Test 2:

    Task 1   92

    Task 2   93

    Task 3   94

Models Answers to Practice Speaking Test 2:

    Model Answer to Task 1   95

    Comments on Model Answer to Task 1   97

    Model Answer to Task 2   99

    Comments on Model Answer to Task 2   101

    Model Answer to Task 3   103

    Comments on Model Answer to Task 3   105

Practice Speaking Test 3:

    Task 1   108

Task 2	109
Task 3	110

Models Answers to Practice Speaking Test 3:

Model Answer to Task 1	111
Comments on Model Answer to Task 1	113
Model Answer to Task 2	115
Comments on Model Answer to Task 2	117
Model Answer to Task 3	119
Comments on Model Answer to Task 3	122

PART 8 – 300 Additional Speaking Practice Test Questions

100 Prompt Cards for IELTS Speaking Task 2	125
200 Speaking Practice Test Questions for Task 3	142
Animals	142
Arts and Crafts	142
Children	142
Clothing	143
Communication	143
Culture and Cultural Events	144
Disagreements	144
Education	145
Environment	145
Family and Friends	146
Food and Nutrition	146
Free Time, Hobbies and Leisure	147
Giving Advice	147

Helping Others	148
Health	148
Humour	149
Jobs and Employment	149
Making Decisions	150
Making Plans	150
Making Promises	151
Memories and Remembering	151
Music and Entertainment	151
Movies	152
News, Media and Technology	152
Public Places	153
Relationships	154
Role Models	154
Social Media	155
Shopping and Consumerism	155
Telephones	156
Television	156
Towns and Cities	157
Transport	157
Travel and Tourism	158
Working Abroad	159

PART 1 – IELTS Speaking Test Overview

IELTS Speaking Test Format

The speaking test is the same for the IELTS Academic and General Training Modules.

Students have a conversation with a certified examiner for the IELTS speaking test.

The speaking test is designed to be interactive and to simulate a real-life discussion as much as possible.

To make the testing experience realistic, the testing topics are designed to elicit discussion between the student and examiner.

However, the student should be able to converse more or less freely and fluently on topics without waiting for the examiner to ask questions.

The entire speaking test will last for 11 to 14 minutes.

Parts of the IELTS Speaking Test

The IELTS speaking test has three parts:

1) Task 1 – The student answers questions on familiar topics. The examiner may ask about the student's family, hobbies or day-to-day life. This part of the speaking test lasts for 3 to 5 minutes.

2) Task 2 – This part of the test is sometimes referred to as "the long turn". The student is expected to speak about a topic for 2 minutes without prompting from the examiner. The student will be provided with a topic card and will then be given one minute to prepare his or her talk. The student can take notes, but should avoid reading from them during his or her response. When the two minutes have passed, the examiner will let the student know. The examiner may also ask questions about the topic when the two minutes have finished.

3) Task 3 – The examiner asks further questions in part 3. These questions will be connected to the topic from part 2, but the part 3 questions will be much more general or abstract. This part of the test can last for up to 5 minutes.

How the IELTS Speaking Test Is Scored

The IELTS speaking test is designed to assess your communication skills in English.

You will be interviewed by a trained IELTS examiner.

He or she will determine whether you can communicate effectively in English by considering the following criteria:

- Fluency and Coherence

    The examiner will assess whether you can speak English naturally, without too many hesitations or long pauses. He or she will also assess whether your communication is clear and easy to understand.

- Lexical Resource

    This part of your score is based on your vocabulary in spoken English. You should aim not only to show that you have an advanced vocabulary level, but also use the vocabulary correctly in your spoken English.

- Grammatical Range and Accuracy

    The examiner will assess whether you can use a range of grammatical structures correctly in your spoken English.

Accordingly, using a variety of verb tenses appropriately in your interview will help you to improve your score.

- Pronunciation

The interviewer will consider how easy it is to understand what you are saying.

How to Prepare for the IELTS Speaking Test

1. **Plan ahead.** This book provides sample topics like you might face on the actual IELTS speaking test. Read through the topics and make notes of the kinds of phrases and responses that you might use for a given topic.

2. **Learn useful phrases for speaking.** Please see our section entitled "Useful Phrases for the Speaking Test" later in this book.

3. **Practise at home.** After you have thought about each of the topics and studied the useful phrases, you should choose a topic and practise speaking about it in front of a mirror. You should not use your notes, but try to speak as freely and fluently as possible. Use a watch and keep track of the time for each section. However, don't over-rehearse. Your examiner will give you a lower score if your response sounds like you have memorised it.

4. **Practise speaking English with friends.** This will help your spoken English to sound more natural and fluent.

4. **Improve your grammar.** Remember that your examiner will be assessing your grammar and sentence construction. You can improve these skills with our publication entitled "IELTS Writing Coursebook with IELTS Grammar Preparation and Language Practice".

5. **Improve your vocabulary.** For a high score on the IELTS speaking test, you will need to show that you know some advanced vocabulary and that you can use the words correctly in sentences. Our publication entitled "IELTS Vocabulary: IELTS Words for the IELTS for Academic Purposes English Test" will help you with this skill.

Tips for Better Performance on Your IELTS Speaking Test

1. **Be sure to answer fully and completely.** You will not be able to demonstrate your language ability if you respond only "yes" or "no", or if you provide only very brief responses to the examiner's questions. For example, if you are asked who you live with, you should not just respond "some friends". Instead, you should respond with complete sentences, such as: "Well, at the moment, I am living with a couple of friends. One of my flatmates is a good friend that I have known since childhood, and the other one is a new friend that I met here while studying on the English foundation course". Notice how the response includes various verb tenses and sentence structures:

I am living – present continuous

is – present simple

I have known – present perfect

met – past simple

while studying – present participle phrase

Responding fully in this way demonstrates that you have confidence and a good command of the English language.

2. **Don't worry about your native accent.** Some students get overly concerned about having a slight accent from their native language when speaking in English. Nevertheless, nearly all non-native speakers of English will speak with an accent. Your accent would only really cause problems if it were so strong that your examiner could not understand you. Remember that the most important thing is to speak clearly and to be understood. If you make a mistake in pronunciation when speaking, don't get flustered. Just correct yourself if you can and continue speaking.

3. **Remember that adjectives can be powerful.** Using simple one-syllable adjectives is very basic and boring. For instance, responding "My friends are nice" is something that a student with one year of English can say. It is much more powerful to use advanced adjectives, such as: "My friends are very *responsible* and *supportive*, but they can also be a little bit *impetuous*, which keeps our friendship exciting".

4. **Speak loudly enough.** Because of cultural differences, students sometimes think that it is better to speak in a quiet tone during the speaking test in order to show respect to the examiner. Yet, in an exam situation, this type of tone can create the impression that a student is timid or lacks confidence. It will also be difficult for the examiner if he or she has to struggle in order to hear you.

5. **Watch your register.** "Register" refers to the level of formality in your language. Many students think that it will be impressive to use phrases that they have heard in movies, but using slang expressions should be avoided because these expressions are very informal.

6. **Watch your speed.** Don't speak too slowly. Your speed should be like a native speaker of English.

7. **Be careful about using words from your native language.** Sometimes students "freeze" on the speaking test because they are thinking of a word in their native language and cannot remember the equivalent word in English. Don't let this happen to you! If you can't think of a word like "enrolment", just apologise and try to explain the meaning by saying something like: "Sorry, I can't remember the word, but it refers to what happens when a student begins a class at university". Then continue speaking.

8. **Don't change the subject.** If you do not stay on the topic that the examiner has set, he or she will think that you have misunderstood the instructions.

PART 2 – Grammar and Verb Tense on Each Task of the Speaking Test

Tasks 1 and 2

On tasks 1 and 2 of the speaking test, you will be asked questions about your day-to-day life, as well as your past or present activities in your current country of residence or your home country.

- **Verb tense for tasks 1 and 2**
  - When discussing these types of activities, you should usually use the present simple, present continuous and present perfect tenses.
  - That is because you will be talking about habitual actions, which requires the present simple.
  - You may also be talking about actions that have a limited duration in the present time, which would require the present continuous.
  - On the other hand, you may be talking about activities of recent significance. In this case, the present perfect tense should be used.
  - You may have the chance to use modal verbs on tasks 1 and 2 of the speaking exam.
  - It is possible to use other verb tenses such as the past simple on these two tasks of the speaking test.
  - For instance, you may be asked to talk about a person who influenced you or a favourite holiday on task 2.

PART 3 – Conditional Sentence Review

Using Conditional Sentences to Improve Your Speaking Test Score

Task 3 of the speaking test turns to topics that are much more complex and difficult than those in tasks 1 and 2.

Therefore, in task 3 of the speaking test, you can demonstrate your grasp of advanced grammatical structures.

Since task 3 of the speaking exam covers speculative topics, the use of conditional sentence structures is very useful on this part of the test.

If you can demonstrate a good command of how to use advanced sentence structures like conditionals, you should be able to raise your score on the speaking test.

We will look at how to use each of the conditionals in the next section of this book.

Please go to the next page, read the information on the different types of conditionals, and then try the exercises at the end of each section.

- If you are speaking about a person who influenced you or a holiday, you will need to use one of the past tenses since you will be describing actions or events that have taken place in the past.
- However, the present simple and present perfect are usually very widely used on tasks 1 and 2.

Task 3

On the third task of the speaking test, you will have a topic that is loosely connected to task 2 of the exam.

For example, if you have been asked to talk about a problem with a flatmate in task 2, you may be asked to talk about conflicts within society in task 3.

- **Conditionals and speculative language on task 3**
  - The topics on task 3 are very general and abstract.
  - These topics will require you to think abstractly and to make generalisations and speculations.
  - Conditional sentences are useful to speculate about past and future events.
  - Using conditional sentences on task 3 will demonstrate that you have a command of advanced English grammar.

We will have a look at conditional sentence structures in the next section.

The Zero Conditional

The zero conditional is used to describe facts and generalisations.

In other words, we use the zero conditional when we want to describe a situation that always has the same outcome or result.

In zero conditional sentences, we can use the word "when" instead of the word "if" without changing the meaning of the sentence.

The zero conditional is formed with the present simple in both the "if clause" and the "main clause" of the sentence.

Also notice that the clauses of the conditional sentences can be inverted.

This means that the positions of the clauses can be swapped.

Examples:

If I go out in the rain, I take my umbrella.

I take my umbrella if I go out in the rain.

When I go out in the rain, I take my umbrella.

I take my umbrella when I go out in the rain.

> Zero conditional:
>
> If . . . + present simple . . . , + present simple

Now try the exercises on the next page.

Zero Conditional – Exercises

Instructions: Form sentences in the zero conditional using the words provided for each sentence. Notice that you may need to add some words when creating each sentence, such as articles and pronouns. Then check your answers on the next page.

1. if / he / not sleep / well / he / be / in a bad mood / next day

_____

2. I / take / train / when / my car/ be / broken down

_____

3. you / look / more intelligent / if / wear / eyeglasses

_____

4. if / you / believe / everything on the internet / you / be / very foolish

_____

5. when / government / create / new laws / society / improve

_____

Zero Conditional – Answers

1. If he does not sleep well, he is in a bad mood the next day.

2. I take the train when my car is broken down.

3. You look more intelligent if you wear eyeglasses.

4. If you believe everything on the internet, you are very foolish.

5. When the government creates new laws, society improves.

The First Conditional

The first conditional is used to describe events that could realistically happen in the future.

It can be used to state plans or intentions or to make predictions.

Plans: I will stay over at her house on Friday if the weather is bad.

Intentions: If I pass my exams, I will go to university.

Predictions: If the company does not monitor its budget, it will have financial problems.

The first conditional is formed with the present simple in the "if clause" and "will + the base form" in the "main clause" of the sentence.

Remember that the clauses of the conditional sentences can be inverted.

This means that the positions of the clauses can be swapped.

Examples:

If I fail my test, I will attend English classes in the evening.

I will attend English classes in the evening if I fail my test.

First conditional:

If . . . + present simple . . . , + will + the base form

Comparing the Zero and First Conditionals

Remember that the zero conditional is used to describe events that happen in general every time they occur.

In contrast, the first conditional is used to describe events that will occur in a particular situation or at a particular time.

Look at the examples below.

Zero conditional:

Economic crisis occurs when inflation and unemployment increase.

First conditional:

Economic crisis will occur if inflation and unemployment increase.

Notice that the zero-conditional sentence above is describing an economic generalisation, but the first-conditional sentence is making a prediction about future economic events.

Now try the exercises on the next page.

First Conditional – Exercises

Instructions: Form sentences in the first conditional using the words provided for each sentence. Notice that you may need to add some words when creating each sentence, such as articles and pronouns. Then check your answers on the next page.

1. if / he / do well / at / interview / he / get / job

   _____

2. if / town council / disapprove of / new supermarket / company / not build / it

   _____

3. staff / get / bonuses / if / work / more efficiently

   _____

4. social problems / become / more serious / if / government / not intervene

   _____

5. people / in my country / be unhappy / if / new members of parliament / not be / honest

   _____

First Conditional – Answers

1. If he does well at the interview, he will get the job.

2. If the town council disapproves of the new supermarket, the company will not build it.

3. The staff will get bonuses if they work more efficiently.

4. Social problems will become more serious if the government does not intervene.

5. People in my country will be unhappy if the new members of parliament are not honest.

The Second Conditional

The second conditional is used to describe events in the present that are impossible because of present circumstances.

Example:

If I knew my teacher's email address, I would send her a message.

The event of sending an email to the teacher is impossible at the present moment because the student does not have the email address.

The second conditional is also used to describe events in the future that are imaginary or extremely improbable.

Example:

If I won a million pounds in the lottery, I would travel around the world in a private jet.

In the preceding sentence, it is extremely improbable that the speaker will win the lottery.

The second conditional is formed with the past simple in the "if clause" and "would + the base form" in the "main clause" of the sentence.

Like all conditional sentences, the clauses in second conditional sentences can be inverted.

Examples:

If I knew my teacher's email address, I would send her a message.

I would send my teacher a message if I knew her email address,

> Second conditional:
>
> If . . . + past simple . . . , + would + the base form

Comparing the First and Second Conditionals

Remember that the first conditional is used to describe events that could realistically happen in the future.

On the other hand, the second conditional is used to describe events that are imaginary, impossible or extremely improbable.

Look at the examples below.

First conditional:

She will lose weight if she watches what she eats.

Second conditional:

She would lose weight if she watched what she ate.

Notice that in the first-conditional sentence, the speaker is confident that her friend will continue to control her calorie intake and lose weight. However, in the second-conditional sentence, the speaker is saying that it is extremely unlikely that her friend will lose weight, perhaps because the speaker has reason to doubt her friend's self-control.

Now try the exercises on the next page.

Second Conditional – Exercises

Instructions: Form sentences in the second conditional using the words provided for each sentence. Notice that you may need to add some words when creating each sentence, such as articles and pronouns. Then check your answers on the next page.

1. if / people / be / more considerate / there / not be / so much / social unrest

   _____

2. if / university / decrease / tuition fees / enrolment / increase

   _____

3. he / be / ecstatic / if / marry / a princess

   _____

4. global warming / improve / if / people / conserve / more energy

   _____

5. more people / go on / holidays abroad / if / airlines / drop / their prices

   _____

Second Conditional – Answers

1. If people were more considerate, there would not be so much social unrest.

2. If the university decreased tuition fees, enrolment would increase.

3. He would be ecstatic if he married a princess.

4. Global warming would improve if people conserved more energy.

5. More people would go on holidays abroad if airlines dropped their prices.

The Third Conditional

The third conditional is used to talk about events in the past.

We use the third conditional to describe events from a retrospective perspective.

In other words, we use this sentence construction to describe how events in the past could have had different results.

The third conditional is formed with the past perfect in the "if clause" and "would have + past participle" in the "main clause" of the sentence.

Remember that the clauses of third conditional sentences can be inverted.

Examples:

He would have passed his exam if he had studied more for it.

If he had studied more for his exam, he would have passed it.

> Third conditional:
>
> If . . . + past perfect . . . , + would have + past participle

Now try the exercises on the next page.

Third Conditional – Exercises

Instructions: Form sentences in the third conditional using the words provided for each sentence. Notice that you may need to add some words when creating each sentence, such as articles and pronouns. Then check your answers on the next page.

1. if / medical authorities / pay more attention / epidemic / not occur

_____

2. if / his company / make more money / he / not claim / bankruptcy

_____

3. housing shortage / not exist / if / more accommodation / be available

_____

4. festivals / in my country / not become / so popular if / parents / not teach / children / about them

_____

5. pollution / worsen / if / people / use / public transport / more often

_____

Third Conditional – Answers

1. If medical authorities had paid pay more attention, the epidemic would not have occurred.

2. If his company had made more money, he would not have claimed bankruptcy.

3. The housing shortage would not have existed if more accommodation had been available.

4. Festivals in my country would not have become so popular if parents had not taught their children about them.

5. Pollution would not have worsened if people had used public transport more often.

Deciding Which Conditional to Use – Exercises

Sometimes students can't decide which conditional is the best to use in certain situations.

Try the exercises below to help you distinguish when to use each type of conditional.

Instructions: You will see the "if clause" for each sentence below. Finish each sentence using the zero, first, second or third conditional, as appropriate.

1. If I pass my exam tomorrow . . .

_____

2. If I hadn't missed the bus yesterday . . .

_____

3. If the employee had not stolen the money . . .

_____

4. If water reaches 100 degrees . . .

_____

5. If the company truly wanted more staff . . .

_____

6. If the weather gets bad later this afternoon . . .

_____

7. If I lived on a deserted island . . .

_____

8. When human beings encounter difficulties in life . . .

_____

Deciding Which Conditional to Use – Answers and Explanations

1. If I pass my exam tomorrow, I will be so happy.

    The word "tomorrow" indicates that we are speaking about the future, so the first conditional is needed in this sentence

2. If I hadn't missed the bus yesterday, I would not have been late to class.

    The word "yesterday" and the use of the past perfect indicate that we need the third conditional structure.

3. If the employee had not stolen the money, she would not have lost her job.

    The use of the past perfect shows that we are speaking retrospectively about a past event, so we need the third conditional structure.

4. If water reaches 100 degrees, it boils.

    The present simple tense shows that we are talking about a scientific generalisation, so we need to use the zero conditional.

5. If the company truly wanted more staff, it would hire them.

    The use of the word "truly" together with the use of the past simple tense indicates that we are speaking about an improbable event. So, we need to use the second conditional.

6. If the weather gets bad later this afternoon, I will not go for a walk.

   The phrase "later this afternoon" indicates that we are speaking about the immediate future, so the first conditional is needed in this sentence

7. If I lived on a deserted island, I would miss my family so much.

   The situation of living on a deserted island is an imaginary one for most people. Accordingly, we need to use the second conditional.

8. When human beings encounter difficulties in life, they often feel discouraged.

   The phrase "human beings" and the use of the present simple show that we are speaking about a generalisation, so we need the zero conditional.

   Now go on to the next section of the study guide, which describes each of the speaking tasks in depth.

PART 4 – Overview of the Three Individual Tasks

Overview of Speaking Task 1

We have talked briefly about task 1 of the IELTS speaking test, but you should know more about the breakdown of each of the individual tasks. This will help you to anticipate each step of each task of the speaking exam.

You will also better understand what to expect on the day of your actual IELTS test when you have a look at the practice speaking tests at the end of this book.

The first task of the IELTS speaking test usually has each of the following steps:

1. The interviewer greets the student and asks him or her to be seated. The examiner then informs the student that the interview will be recorded.

2. The interviewer begins by asking the student to state his or her full name. The interviewer also requests to see the student's identification.

3. The examiner asks the student to introduce him- or herself and to state his or her country of origin.

4. The examiner asks the student questions on one or more familiar topics. This part of the test normally consists of three to five questions and covers one or two topics.

How to Prepare for Speaking Task 1

1) **Think about what you already know about familiar topics.** If you think about your hometown, family, hobbies and friends, you can anticipate the kinds of questions that the examiner might ask you.

2) **Check your vocabulary.** Be sure that you know all of the vocabulary that you need in order to describe your hometown and hobbies.

3) **Improve your fluency.** You will be more fluent on the day of your test if you have thought about your answers in advance and have practised speaking about them with a friend.

4) **Use a variety of verb tenses.** Remember that the present simple, present continuous and present perfect can be used to answer questions on task 1 of the test.

Speaking Task 1 – Sample Response and Exercise

Instructions: Have a look at the following sample dialogue between a student and an IELTS examiner. Underline the verbs and identify the verb tenses that the student uses. Then check your answers on the next page.

Examiner: In the first part of the test, I'm going to ask you questions about yourself. So, tell me a little bit about your hometown. Can you describe it for me?

Student: Yes, actually it is quite a small, little village. It is located about 50 kilometres from the capital city, and my family has lived there for more than thirty years. We have been very content living there since my father works nearby and my mother works from home.

Examiner: What would you say is the best aspect of this particular place . . . this location?

Student: Well, I would say that the best thing is that my siblings are attending an excellent school at the moment. They are really only able to do that because my family resides in the area.

Examiner: So, you think that your hometown is a good place to live?

Student: Oh yes, apart from the great school, the people in the town are really welcoming and neighbourly. They will help out any stranger in need of assistance because it is just in their nature to be that way.

Examiner: Okay, we will change the topic a little now. I wonder if you could tell me a bit about your accommodation.

Student: I am living in a shared flat right now with five other students, so the atmosphere is a bit chaotic at times, but on the whole, I am really enjoying my stay in the flat, and I am getting to know a lot of new people.

Speaking Task 1 – Answer to the Exercise

The verbs that the student uses have been underlined in the dialogue below. The verb tense is provided in brackets after each verb.

Examiner: In the first part of the test, I'm going to ask you questions about yourself. So, tell me a little bit about your hometown. Can you describe it for me?

Student: Yes, actually it <u>is</u> [present simple] quite a small, little village. It <u>is</u> [present simple] located about 50 kilometres from the capital city, and my family <u>has lived</u> [present perfect] there for more than thirty years. We <u>have been</u> [present perfect] very content living there since my father <u>works</u> [present simple] nearby and my mother <u>works</u> [present simple] from home.

Examiner: What would you say is the best aspect of this particular place . . . this location?

Student: Well, I would say that the best thing is that my siblings <u>are attending</u> [present continuous] an excellent school at the moment. They really <u>are</u> [present simple] able to do that only because my family <u>resides</u> [present simple] in the area.

Examiner: So, you think that your hometown is a good place to live?

Student: Oh yes, apart from the great school, the people in the town <u>are</u> [present simple] really welcoming and neighbourly. They <u>will help out</u> [will

+ base form] any stranger in need of assistance because it <u>is</u> [present simple] just in their nature to be that way.

Examiner: Okay, we will change the topic a little now. I wonder if you could tell me a bit about your accommodation.

Student: I <u>am living</u> [present continuous] in a shared flat right now with five other students, so the atmosphere <u>is</u> [present simple] a bit chaotic at times, but on the whole, I <u>am really enjoying</u> [present continuous] my stay in the flat, and I <u>am getting acquainted</u> [present continuous] with a lot of new people.

Overview of Speaking Task 2

As mentioned previously, task two of the IELTS speaking test is referred to as the long turn. Task 2 of the test consists of the following steps:

1. The examiner gives a prompt card to the student. The prompt card contains information on a certain topic. The card is called a "prompt card" because it is designed to prompt or assist you in thinking of potential responses to the topic.

2. Remember that you will have one minute to prepare after you receive the prompt card.

3. You then will need to talk for two minutes without the examiner asking you any questions. You can talk about your own life experiences in task 2 of the test, so try to relax and make your talk as interesting as possible.

4. The examiner will inform you when two minutes have passed.

5. The examiner may ask you a question about what you have said in task 2 before moving on to task 3 of the speaking test.

How to Prepare for Speaking Task 2

1) **Make some notes on familiar topics.** Practise making notes on familiar topics, using abbreviations and symbols to help you jot down your ideas quickly. Remember that you can make notes during the one-minute preparation part of the test, but you should not rely on your notes since reading directly from them will make your speech sound unnatural.

For example, if a student was asked to describe one of his or favourite places, his or her notes might look like this:

Cabo de Gata > S. Spain

My fav b/c on sea

Fam hols in sum

He or she would then say something like this:

Cabo de Gata in southern Spain is my favourite place because it is on the sea. I have fond memories of this place because my family had holidays there every summer.

2) **Practise speaking for two-minute time periods.** Before taking the actual IELTS speaking test, you should practise speaking on topics for two minutes at a time. As you practise speaking, you should pace yourself and watch the clock to be sure that you can speak for the required amount of time.

3) **Record yourself to monitor your performance.** Record yourself and then play the recording back and listen to yourself talking. Pay attention to your talking speed, as well as your pronunciation and vocabulary.

Speaking Task 2 – Sample Response and Exercise

Here is a sample prompt card like you will receive on task 2 of the IELTS speaking test.

> Describe your favourite place.
>
> Think about:
>
> - Whether it is a room, building, monument, city, holiday location or another place.
> - Why you like it.
> - What comes to mind when you think about this place.

Instructions: Now have a look at the following sample long turn for task 2. Underline the verbs and identify the verb tenses that the student uses. Then check your answers on the next page.

Student: Cabo de Gata in southern Spain is my favourite place because it is on the sea. I have fond memories of this place since my family had holidays there every summer when I was a small child. Actually, Cabo de Gata is a popular holiday destination because it is a natural park, so it has protected areas for birds and learning centres where a person can find out more about the ecology of the area. The bird sanctuary is a fantastic place that has a peaceful atmosphere, and you can see the most incredible species of birds and other wildlife there. Another aspect of this place that I really enjoy is the fact that it combines all of the features of the landscape that I love the most. I mean, you can look at the mountains from the beach because the park is located on the coast, and it is near geological formations of volcanic rock. In fact, although it was done a few years ago, the "Indiana Jones" movie was filmed in front of one of the cliffs in the park. I also enjoy the activities that you can take part in at the park. I have walked on the trails in the park many times, and I have also snorkelled and camped there. When I think about this place, I have such fond memories of my childhood that I begin to feel quite nostalgic about it. In fact, I am feeling a bit homesick as I describe it to you.

Speaking Task 2 – Answer to the Exercise

The verbs that the student uses have been underlined in the dialogue below. The verb tense is provided in brackets after each verb.

Student: Cabo de Gata in southern Spain is [present simple] my favourite place because it is [present simple] on the sea. I have [present simple] fond memories of this place since my family had [past simple] holidays there every summer when I was [past simple] a small child. Actually, Cabo de Gata is [present simple] a popular holiday destination because it is [present simple] a natural park, so it has [present simple] protected areas for birds and learning centres where a person can find out [modal + base form phrasal verb] more about the ecology of the area. The bird sanctuary is [present simple] a fantastic place that has [present simple] a peaceful atmosphere, and you can see [modal + base form] the most incredible species of birds and other wildlife there. Another aspect of this place that I really enjoy is the fact that it combines [present simple] all of the features of the landscape that I love [present simple] the most. I mean, you can look [modal + base form] at the mountains from the beach because the park is [present simple] located on the coast, and it is [present simple] near geological formations of volcanic rock. In fact, although it was done [past simple – passive] a few years ago, the "Indiana Jones" movie was filmed [past simple – passive] in front of one of the cliffs in the park. I also enjoy [present simple] the activities that you can take part in [modal + base form phrasal verb] at the park. I have walked [present perfect] on the trails in the park many times, and I have also snorkelled and camped [present perfect] there. When I think about this place, I have [present simple] such fond memories of my childhood that I begin to feel [present simple + infinitive] quite nostalgic about it. In fact, I am feeling [present continuous] a bit homesick as I describe [present simple] it to you.

Overview of Speaking Task 3

As mentioned previously, task three of the IELTS speaking test is where you need to speak about general or abstract concepts. Task 3 of the test consists of the following steps:

1. The examiner indicates that you are moving into the final part of the exam by saying something like: "Okay, now we are going to move to the third part of the test".

2. The examiner will then try to elicit responses from you on more complex topics. Questions on this part of the exam are usually of three of four different types. You may be asked to:

    a. describe a person, place or situation

    b. compare one or more things

    c. discuss a possible solution to a problem

    d. speculate or make a prediction about the future

3. The examiner's questions will become more difficult as you progress through this part of the exam.

4. Finally, the examiner will end your interview by saying something like; "Thank you. That is the end of the speaking test".

How to Prepare for Speaking Task 3

1) **Learn how to describe, compare and speculate.** You should have a look at the "Useful Phrases" and "Vocabulary Usage" sections of this book. In particular, you should study the words in the "People" and "Places" sections of the "Vocabulary Usage" unit later in this book to help you remember how to give spoken descriptions during your exam. You should also study the phrases for comparing, contrasting and speculating, and learn how to use these phrases if you do not know them already.

2) **Improve your knowledge of conditional sentence structures.** Speculating and making predictions can perhaps be best done by using one of the conditional sentence structures. Please refer back to the conditional sentence structure sections in this publication to review your skills in this area.

3) **Improve your vocabulary.** The use of advanced vocabulary is especially important on task 3 of the speaking test. You should therefore study the word lists provided in this book.

4) **Practise with some sample topics.** Although it is impossible to know what exact questions you will be asked on the day of your test, you can improve your language skills by trying the practice tests and looking at the sample responses at the end of this book.

Speaking Task 3 – Sample Response and Exercise

Instructions: Now have a look at the following conversation between a student and an examiner. Then underline the conditional sentence structures and identify the types of conditionals that the student uses. Check your answers on the next page.

Examiner: We've been taking about places and buildings in the second part of the test. Now I'd like to ask you a few more questions in this area. In your country, how are monuments and historic places treated?

Student: In general, people regard monuments with great respect. For example, people tend to venerate memorials to soldiers who have fallen in various wars. On the other hand, the case of historic buildings is a bit more difficult, and the government is now attempting to introduce measures to protect historic structures.

Examiner: So, that is something new in your country?

Student: What I mean is that, in the past, there was a tendency to demolish old buildings in order to make way for newer, modern structures, but nowadays, people are beginning to realise that older structures literally house the cultural heritage of our country. People are also trying to come to terms with the fact that if they hadn't been so hasty in demolishing these structures in the past, we would not have got to the point in the present of needing to pass laws to protect these architectural treasures.

Examiner: So, what do you think are some possible solutions to that problem?

Student: Research shows that when the government provides money for restoration projects, people's views on public spending improve. So, if cost wasn't such a problem, the government would fund more of these types of restoration projects.

Examiner: I see. So, is it better to protect old buildings or to construct new ones?

Student: Well, it depends on your perspective. I guess building materials for restoration projects can be incredibly expensive, and some modern buildings can be sympathetically constructed in order to appear older than they really are.

Examiner: Do you think that historical buildings will become more important to a country's culture in the future?

Student: I think that in the future, it could be the case that historical buildings will become more important. The fact is that many historical buildings have already been torn down, so it is more likely that the historic structures that remain standing will become more precious and important to a country's culture.

Examiner: Thank you. That is the end of the speaking test.

Speaking Task 3 – Answer to the Exercise

The conditional sentences that the student uses have been underlined in the dialogue below. The type of conditional is provided in brackets after each sentence.

Examiner: We've been taking about places and buildings in the second part of the test. Now I'd like to ask you a few more questions in this area. In your country, how are monuments and historic places treated?

Student: In general, people regard monuments with great respect. For example, people tend to venerate memorials to soldiers who have fallen in various wars. On the other hand, the case of historic buildings is a bit more difficult, and the government is now attempting to introduce measures to protect historic structures.

Examiner: So, that is something new in your country?

Student: What I mean is that, in the past, there was a tendency to demolish old buildings in order to make way for newer, modern structures, but nowadays, people are beginning to realise that older structures literally house the cultural heritage of our country. People are also trying to come to terms with the fact that <u>if they *hadn't been* so hasty in demolishing these structures in the past, we *would not have got* to the point in the</u>

present of needing to pass laws to protect these architectural treasures. [third conditional]

Examiner: So, what do you think are some possible solutions to that problem?

Student: Research shows that when the government *provides* money for restoration projects, people's views on public spending *improve*. [zero conditional] So, if cost *wasn't such* a problem, the government *would fund* more of these types of restoration projects. [second conditional]

Examiner: I see. So, is it better to protect old buildings or to construct new ones?

Student: Well, it depends on your perspective. I guess building materials for restoration projects can be incredibly expensive, and some modern buildings can be sympathetically constructed in order to appear older than they really are.

Examiner: Do you think that historical buildings will become more important to a country's culture in the future?

Student: I think that in the future, it could be the case that historical buildings will become more important. The fact is that many historical buildings have already been torn down, so it is more likely that the historic structures that remain standing will become more precious and important to a country's culture.

Examiner: Thank you. That is the end of the speaking test.

PART 5 – Useful Phrases for the Speaking Test

This section contains useful phrases for the IELTS speaking exam. The phrases have been placed into categories, according to the functions that you will need to use on the real IELTS speaking test. You should study the following lists and try to use these words as you respond to the sample exercises later in this book.

Phrases for talking about the present

at present

at the moment

every day

nowadays

right now

so far

until now

Phrases for talking about the past

I got accustomed to (something / doing something).

I got used to (doing something).

I used to (do something).

Phrases for collecting your thoughts

Anyway, . . .

As I said before, . . .

As I was saying, . . .

In any event, . . .

So, . . .

The thing is . . .

Well . . .

What I am trying to say is that . . .

Phrases for emphasising

Actually, . . .

In fact, . . .

The fact is that . . .

To be honest, . . .

. . . really . . .

Phrases for explaining what you mean

I mean, . . .

I mean that . . .

In other words, . . .

What I mean is . . .

Phrases for giving examples

For example, . . .

For instance, . . .

In particular, . . .

Phrases for expressing your own opinion

I believe that . . .

I can't be bothered (to do something).

I enjoy it because . . .

I don't like (something / to do something).

I don't think that . . .

I think that . . .

I prefer . . .

I would consider it to be a good idea if . . .

I wouldn't want to . . .

In my opinion, . . .

My view is that . . .

Personally, . . .

The way I see it . . .

Phrases for talking about others' opinions

Some hold the view that . . .

Some people believe that . . .

Other people have the opinion that . . .

Others think that . . .

People are beginning to realise that . . .

People seem to think that . . .

Phrases for giving generalisations

as a rule

for the most part

generally speaking

in general

in most cases

on the whole

Phrases for comparing and contrasting

alternatively

apart from

compared to

in contrast to

instead of

just like

on the contrary

on the other hand

rather than

Phrases for describing and explaining

Another aspect is . . .

Apart from that, . . .

. . . due to the fact that . . .

It is a beautiful / amazing / fantastic place.

The most noticeable aspect is that . . .

One of the most important features is . . .

One reason is that . . .

Phrases for giving advice

I would advise you (to do something).

If I were you, I would . . .

The best thing would be to . . .

Phrases for speculating and predicting

Hopefully, . . .

I guess . . .

I guess it could be that . . .

I hope that . . .

I imagine that . . .

I suppose . . .

I suppose that . . .

I suspect that . . .

If possible, I'd like to see . . .

In the future, . . .

It could be the case that . . .

It depends on your perspective.

It is more likely that . . .

It is possible that . . .

It might be that . . .

It seems that . . .

It seems to be that . . .

One can expect that . . .

People seem to be happy (to do something).

People tend to . . .

We can assume that . . .

We should plan to . . .

PART 6 – Vocabulary Usage on the Speaking Test

This section contains useful words for the IELTS speaking exam. The words have been placed into categories, according to the subjects that have most commonly appeared on past IELTS examinations. You should study the following lists and try to use these words as you respond to the sample exercises later in this book.

<u>Culture and Society</u>

civilisation

conflict

culturally acceptable

culturally insular

culture shock

diversity

globalisation

misconceptions

stereotypes

<u>Education</u>

certificate

co-educational schools

coursework

curriculum

degree

diploma

educator

graduate

higher education

IT ("information technology")

lecturer

online degrees

primary education

qualifications

secondary education

Environment

climate change

environmentally friendly

global warming

pollution

public transport

traffic jams

Family, Friends and Colleagues

acquaintance

friend

best friend

boss

colleague

employee

employer

fiancé

fiancée

neighbour

partner

to feel homesick

to get nostalgic

to instil (something in someone)

to miss home

to miss someone

Food and Nutrition

bitter

rancid

savoury

sweet

tart

calorie intake

contaminated water

food groups

good nutrition

healthy diet

to be malnourished

to become overweight

to get food poisoning

to go hungry

to overeat

Free Time, Hobbies and Leisure

bowling

camping

collecting

cooking

cycling

gardening

hiking

playing a musical instrument

to avoid getting burnt out

to be a homebody

to be an avid reader

to be an enthusiast (of an activity)

to enjoy peace and quiet

to go out to eat

to go to a football match

to keep fit

to play a sport

to surf the internet

to watch a movie

Historical Buildings

architectural techniques

building materials

conservation

cultural heritage

demolition

dilapidated

historic landmark

listed building

monuments

new-build

restoration

sympathetically restored

unsightly

Housing

detached house

eviction

housing benefit

private housing

public housing

repossession

semi-detached house

shanty town

slums

social housing

suburban

suburbs

terraced house

urban

Newspapers, Media and Technology

broadcast media

broadsheet newspapers

journalist

landline telephone

media bias

the newsagent's

newspaper headlines

newspaper reports

online media

printed media

sensationalism

social progress

tabloid newspaper

technological advance

technological breakthrough

technological development

technological innovation

technological revolution

to be glued to your mobile device

to subscribe to a newspaper

People – Adjectives

amiable

approachable

arrogant

conservative

down-to-earth

duplicitous

hard-working

hedonistic

impulsive

inspiring

liberal

motivating

neighbourly

presentable

reprehensible

repulsive

respectable

self-centred

warm-hearted

welcoming

well-mannered

Places – Phrases and Adjectives

It has a(n) + adjective atmosphere.

It is a(n) + adjective place.

It is a bit + adjective.

Adjectives:

bustling

calm

chaotic

charming

crowded

fascinating

lively

peaceful

picturesque

popular

touristy

Relationships - Verbs

to be on a first name basis with someone

to become friends with someone

to get acquainted with someone

to get on with someone

to start a relationship with someone

to end a relationship with someone

to get engaged to someone

to get married to someone

to marry someone

to get divorced from someone

Shopping

advertising slogan

brand loyalty

brand names

consumer

consumerism

consumer goods

credit card

feel-good factor

materialism

online shopping

outdoor marketing

product placement

returns policy

uncontrolled spending

viral marketing

to be a spendthrift

to be careful with money

to be frugal

to be stingy

Social Problems

alcoholism

crime

cyber bullying

domestic abuse

drug abuse

intolerance

poverty

prejudice

racism

sexism

substance abuse

terrorism

Television

chat show

cookery programmes

flat-screen TV

game show

newscast

paid programmes

reality TV programmes

remote control

reruns

sitcoms

soap opera

state television

wide-screen TV

Transport

bicycle lanes

bus

bus stop

free bus pass

cable car

cars

commuting

pedestrian

taxi

taxi stand

traffic congestion

train

train station

underground

vehicles

Travel and Tourism

the holiday of a lifetime

holiday destination

holiday resort

hordes of tourists

package holiday

preservation

self-catering

souvenirs

stunning views

tourist attractions

to go on a long weekend

to go on holiday

to go out of season

to go sightseeing

to learn local customs

PART 7 – Practice Speaking Tests with Model Answers

PRACTICE SPEAKING TEST 1 – TASK 1

The examiner asks the candidate familiar questions about him- or herself, work, studies or hobbies.

EXAMPLE

Can you tell me something about:

- your family members
- your friends
- your home country

PRACTICE SPEAKING TEST 1 – TASK 2

The examiner will give you some information on a topic. You will have two minutes to talk about the topic. You will have one minute beforehand to prepare for your talk. You can make notes to help you prepare if you so wish.

> I would like you to think about a person who has had an influence on you.
>
> Talk about:
>
> - Why you remember them.
>
> - How you would describe his or her personality.
>
> - How they influenced you.

PRACTICE SPEAKING TEST 1 – TASK 3

Discussion topics:

The importance of role models

Example questions:

Describe the qualities of a good role model.

Compare the differences between a good role model and a bad one.

Present an example of a poor role model.

Evaluate the effects of poor role models.

Role models and their place in society

Example questions:

Discuss how role models have changed in society over time.

Describe the extent to which the media creates and destroys role models.

Speculate about how society's role models may change in the future.

MODEL ANSWER TEST 1 – TASK 1

Examiner: In the first part of the speaking test, we are going to talk about your family and friends. First of all, can you tell me a little bit about your family?

Student: Well, I am from a family that would probably be considered fairly large by most people. I have three brothers and two sisters. My mother and dad live in the family home, of course, and my father's parents also live with us. Actually, I really enjoy living in such a busy household.

Examiner: How would you describe your parents and grandparents?

Student: Probably the most noticeable aspect of their personalities is that they are very well-mannered and hard-working people, and that is something that all of them have tried to instil in me.

Examiner: Can you also tell me something about your friends?

Student: I have a best friend and two other really good friends, and we used to see each other at school and on the weekends. While my parents are more conservative, my friends can be a bit impulse at times, which is why I enjoy being with them, I suppose.

Examiner: Have you meet any new people here on the course?

Student: Oh yes, I have made quite a few new friends and acquaintances here on the course, and I am meeting more new people every day, but still, I miss my friends back home, too.

Examiner: What other things do your miss about your home country?

Student: In particular, I miss the food! But I have found a really good supermarket here in town that sells some products from my home country, so that helps.

COMMENTS ON MODEL ANSWER TEST 1 – TASK 1

Comments: The verbs that the student uses have been underlined in the dialogue. The verb tense is provided in brackets after each verb.

Examiner: In the first part of the speaking test, we are going to talk about your family and friends. First of all, can you tell me a little bit about your family?

Student: Well, I am [present simple] from a family that would probably be [modal verb] considered fairly large by most people. I have [present simple] three brothers and two sisters. My mother and dad live [present simple] in the family home, of course, and my father's parents also live [present simple] with us. Actually, I really enjoy [present simple] living in such a busy household.

Examiner: How would you describe your parents and grandparents?

Student: Probably the most noticeable aspect of their personalities is [present simple] that they are [present simple] very well-mannered and hard-working people, and that is [present simple] something that all of them have tried to instil [present perfect + infinitive] in me.

Examiner: Can you also tell me something about your friends?

Student: I have [present simple] a best friend and two other really good friends, and we used to see [used to do] each other at school and on the weekends. While my parents are [present simple] more conservative, my friends can be [modal verb] a bit impulse at times, which is [present simple] why I enjoy [present simple] being with them, I suppose.

Examiner: Have you meet any new people here on the course?

Student: Oh yes, I have made [present perfect] quite a few new friends and acquaintances here on the course, and I am meeting [present continuous] more new people every day, but still, I miss [present simple] my friends back home, too.

Examiner: What other things do your miss about your home country?

Student: In particular, I miss [present simple] the food! But I have found [present perfect] a really good supermarket here in town that sells [present simple] some products from my home country, so that helps [present simple].

MODEL ANSWER TEST 1 – TASK 2

Here is the prompt card again for your reference:

> I would like you to think about a person who has had an influence on you.
>
> Talk about:
>
> - Why you remember them.
>
> - How you would describe his or her personality.
>
> - How they influenced you.

Student: The person who had the most influence on me was a piano teacher that I had when I was a small child. My parents really wanted me to learn how to play a musical instrument when I was little, even though I was more interested in playing sports and running around outside, to be honest. So, my parents bought this beautiful piano for me to play, and the piano is still in their living room to this day. In any event, my teacher was called Mrs. Lee, and she used to come to my family home every Tuesday to give me a piano lesson. I suspect that Mrs. Lee knew that I would have preferred to be outside playing because she was such a warm-hearted and down-to-earth person, and she had children of her own, too. But in spite of my lack of any genuine interest in the subject, she managed to make the lessons fun and to motivate me. She had a big influence on me because she taught me that sometimes it is better to please others, instead of pleasing yourself. I mean, my parents have done so much for me in my life, and looking back, I am glad that I did what they wanted me to do, since I made them happy by playing the piano. I am still a bit selfish at times, and I do some things that are just for my own enjoyment, but learning how to make other people happy was an important life lesson for me.

COMMENTS ON MODEL ANSWER TEST 1 – TASK 2

Comments: The verbs that the student uses have been underlined in the dialogue. The verb tense is provided in brackets after each verb. Notice that if you are asked to describe a person who influenced you, you are more likely to use some form of the past tense, since you will be describing an influence that took place in the past. Also notice the adjectives, provided in *italics*, which are used to describe the person.

Student: The person who had [past simple] the most influence on me was [past simple] a piano teacher that I had [past simple] when I was [past simple] a small child. My parents really wanted [past simple] me to learn how to play a musical instrument when I was [past simple] little, even though I was [past simple] more interested in playing sports and running around outside, to be honest. So, my parents bought [past simple] this beautiful piano for me to play, and the piano is [present simple] still in their living room to this day. In any event, my teacher was called [past simple – passive] Mrs. Lee, and she used to come [used to do] to my family home every Tuesday to give me a piano lesson. I suspect [present simple] that Mrs. Lee knew [past simple] that I would have preferred [modal + present perfect] to be outside playing because she was [past simple] such *a warm-hearted* and *down-to-earth* person, and she had [past simple] children of her own, too. But in spite of my lack of any genuine interest in the subject, she managed to make [past simple + infinitive] the lessons fun and to motivate me. She had [past simple] a big influence on me because she taught [past simple] me that sometimes it is [present simple] better to please others, instead of pleasing yourself. I mean, my parents have done [present perfect] so much for me in my life, and looking back, I am [present simple] glad that I did [past simple] what they wanted [past simple] me to do, since I made [past simple] them happy by playing the piano. I am [present simple] still a bit selfish at times, and I do [present simple] some things that are just for my own enjoyment, but learning how to make other people happy was [past simple] an important life lesson for me.

MODEL ANSWER TEST 1 – TASK 3

Examiner: We have been talking about a person who influenced you. Now I'd like to talk about role models in general. Could you describe the qualities of a good role model?

Student: A good role model should be an inspiring and motivating person because, of course, if a person is a good leader, he or she will inspire others to do great things, too. So, when role models excel in their lives, other people want to emulate their actions.

Examiner: Can you compare the differences between a good role model and a bad one?

Student: One can expect that a good role model will be a respectable person, in contrast to a poor role model, who may be a very hedonistic and self-centred person. The good role model will also be an amiable and approachable person, but a poor model might have repulsive behaviour, so people may not even want to get to know the poor role model.

Examiner: Have role models have changed in society over time?

Student: Yes, I believe that they have changed, and that phenomenon is mostly due to the fact that there is a lot more information about people nowadays on the internet, especially on platforms like You Tube and Facebook and so on. If so much information wasn't available about celebrities, the public wouldn't know as much about famous people and other role models. So, role models in modern society have to be more careful about their behaviour than role models in the past. Alternatively, a role model in modern society would need to be kind of duplicitous and live a double life. In other words, they would have a public persona, but then behave differently in private.

Examiner: Can you describe the extent to which the media creates and destroys role models?

Student: As I was saying, social media is having an enormous impact on public figures at present. It seems that the media helps to build people up and make them popular, but then public opinion sometimes turns against the celebrity, and members of the public can use social media to cut down or criticise the public figure. So, what I am trying to say is that in most cases, the media is a vehicle for both creating and destroying the role model.

Examiner: Can you speculate about how society's role models may change in the future?

Student: I hope that in the future public figures will be known for making important advancements for society. I think it's lamentable that a lot of our current celebrities are brought to public attention by participating in reality TV programmes, instead of having done something helpful for society.

Examiner: Thank you. That is the end of the test.

COMMENTS ON MODEL ANSWER TEST 1 – TASK 3

Comments: The conditional sentences that the student uses have been underlined in the dialogue below. The type of conditional is provided in brackets after each sentence. Also notice the adjectives, provided in *italics*, which are used to describe the person and his or her behaviour. Finally, you should study the useful phrases, provided in **bold**.

Examiner: We have been talking about a person who influenced you. Now I'd like to talk about role models in general. Could you describe the qualities of a good role model?

Student: A good role model should be an *inspiring* and *motivating* person because, of course, <u>if a person is a good leader, he or she will inspire others to do great things</u> [first conditional], too. So, <u>when role models excel in their lives, other people want to emulate their actions</u> [zero conditional].

Examiner: Can you compare the differences between a good role model and a bad one?

Student: **One can expect that** a good role model will be a *respectable* person, **in contrast to** a poor role model, who may be a very *hedonistic* and *self-centred* person. The good role model will also be an *amiable* and *approachable* person, but a poor model might have *repulsive* behaviour, so people may not even want to get to know the poor role model.

Examiner: Have role models have changed in society over time?

Student: Yes, **I believe that** they have changed, and that phenomenon is mostly **due to the fact that** there is a lot more information about people nowadays on the internet, especially on platforms like You Tube and Facebook and so on. <u>If so much information wasn't available about celebrities, the public wouldn't know as much about famous people and other role models</u> [second conditional]. So, role models in modern society have to be more careful about their behaviour than role models in the past. **Alternatively**, a role model in modern society would need to be kind of *duplicitous* and live a double life. **In other words**, they would have a public persona, but then behave differently in private.

Examiner: Can you describe the extent to which the media creates and destroys role models?

Student: **As I was saying**, social media is having an enormous impact on public figures at present. **It seems that** the media helps to build people up and make them popular, but then public opinion sometimes turns against the celebrity, and members of the public can use social media to cut down or criticise the public figure. So, **what I am trying to say** is that **in most**

cases, the media is a vehicle for both creating and destroying the role model.

Examiner: Can you speculate about how society's role models may change in the future?

Student: **I hope that** in the future public figures will be known for making important advancements for society. **I think** it's lamentable that a lot of our current celebrities are brought to public attention by participating in reality TV programmes, instead of having done something helpful for society.

Examiner: Thank you. That is the end of the test.

PRACTICE SPEAKING TEST 2 – TASK 1

The examiner asks the candidate familiar questions about him- or herself, work, studies or hobbies.

EXAMPLE

Can you tell me something about:

- your interests or hobbies
- your favourite way to spend the weekend
- your holidays

PRACTICE SPEAKING TEST 2 – TASK 2

The examiner will give you some information on a topic. You will have two minutes to talk about the topic. You will have one minute beforehand to prepare for your talk. You can make notes to help you prepare if you so wish.

> I would like you to describe a national festival or celebration in your country.
>
> Talk about:
>
> - When it is celebrated.
>
> - How and why it is celebrated.

PRACTICE SPEAKING TEST 2 – TASK 3

Discussion topics:

The importance of national festivals

Example questions:

Describe the importance of national festivals.

Compare the differences between a festival in your country with one in another country.

Evaluate the effects of international festivals.

National festivals and social change

Example questions:

Discuss how international festivals have changed over time.

Analyse the extent to which international festivals influence the future of a host country.

Speculate about how festivals might change in the future.

MODEL ANSWER TEST 2 – TASK 1

Examiner: In this first part of the test, I am going to ask you some questions about yourself. Can you tell me a little bit about how you like to spend your free time?

Student: Yes, I like to play football, so I usually play with a group of my friends every Wednesday afternoon. Apart from that, I also like to surf the internet when I am relaxing in my accommodation in the evening. So, I guess I could say that I like to be active and keep fit, but I also enjoy peace and quiet, too.

Examiner: Do you have any other hobbies?

Student: Well, I go to the cinema on occasion, but really, I am more of a homebody, so I prefer watching movies at home.

Examiner: What is your favourite way to spend the weekend?

Student: I think like most students, the majority of my time on the weekend is spent studying. But, on Saturday evening, my friends and I take a break, and we cook a meal together. That is probably my favourite part of the week because we prepare recipes from my home country, and we have such a good time eating and chatting with each other.

Examiner: Okay, we will change the topic slightly now. Could you tell me something about your holidays?

Student: I haven't gone on many holidays, but the last time I went on one, my family and I visited such a fantastic place. It was a cultural museum in a nearby town, and I really loved looking at all of the exhibits and learning more about my home country.

COMMENTS ON MODEL ANSWER TEST 2 – TASK 1

Comments: The verbs that the student uses have been underlined in the dialogue. The verb tense is provided in brackets after each verb.

Examiner: In this first part of the test, I am going to ask you some questions about yourself. Can you tell me a little bit about how you like to spend your free time?

Student: Yes, I like to play [present simple + infinitive] football, so I usually play [present simple] with a group of my friends every Wednesday afternoon. Apart from that, I also like to surf [present simple + infinitive] the internet when I am relaxing [present continuous] in my accommodation in the evening. So, I guess I could say that I like to be [present simple + infinitive] active and keep fit, but I also enjoy [present simple] peace and quiet, too.

Examiner: Do you have any other hobbies?

Student: Well, I go [present simple] to the cinema on occasion, but really, I am [present simple] more of a homebody, so I prefer [present simple] watching movies at home.

Examiner: What is your favourite way to spend the weekend?

Student: I think like most students, the majority of my time on the weekend is spent [present simple – passive] studying. But, on Saturday evening, my friends and I take [present simple] a break, and we cook [present simple] a meal together. That is [present simple] probably my favourite part of the week because we prepare [present simple] recipes from my home country, and we have [present simple] such a good time eating and chatting with each other.

Examiner: Okay, we will change the topic slightly now. Could you tell me something about your holidays?

Student: I haven't gone [present perfect] on many holidays, but the last time I went [past simple] on one, my family and I visited [past simple] such a fantastic place. It was [past simple] a cultural museum in a nearby town, and I really loved [past simple] looking at all of the exhibits and learning more about my home country.

MODEL ANSWER TEST 2 – TASK 2

Here is the prompt card again for your reference:

I would like you to describe a national festival or celebration in your country.

Talk about:

- When it is celebrated.

- How and why it is celebrated.

Student: May Day is one of the most important celebrations in my country. May Day is celebrated on the first day of May each year, and it is supposed to be the day that employees get to have a day off in acknowledgement of their hard work throughout the rest of the year. May Day was celebrated more widely in the past than it is now, because some shops are actually open on this holiday nowadays, so that means that not everybody gets to have the day off work to relax. Villages used to have parades and special traditional dances to celebrate the day, but those sorts of events are becoming less popular since some young people live so far away from home, and because some people have to work on the day, as I mentioned earlier. Most families get together with each other to celebrate this holiday, and if the weather is good, they have picnics or barbecues in order to enjoy the outdoors. I guess people really love eating outside, especially if they have to be inside during the week at an office job. In my family, for instance, we go out to my grandfather's cottage in the countryside the night before. Then, the next morning we get up and set a table outside and get some food ready. We spend the day chatting with each other, and my grandma makes a cake as a special treat that we eat later in the day. We have celebrated the holiday like this for as long as I can remember. Actually, I am really looking forward to celebrating the day with my family again when I return to my country at the end of this course.

COMMENTS ON MODEL ANSWER TEST 2 – TASK 2

Comments: The verbs that the student uses have been underlined in the dialogue. The verb tense is provided in brackets after each verb.

Student: May Day is [present simple] one of the most important celebrations in my country. May Day is celebrated [present simple – passive] on the first day of May each year, and it is supposed to be [present simple – passive + infinitive] the day that employees get to have [present simple + infinitive] a day off in acknowledgement of their hard work throughout the rest of the year. May Day was celebrated [past simple – passive] more widely in the past than it is [present simple] now, because some shops are [present simple] actually open on this holiday nowadays, so that means that not everybody gets to have [present simple + infinitive] the day off work to relax. Villages used to have [used to do] parades and special traditional dances to celebrate the day, but those sorts of events are becoming [present continuous] less popular since some young people live [present simple] so far away from home, and because some people have to work [present simple + infinitive] on the day, as I mentioned earlier. Most families get together [present simple – phrasal verb] with each other to celebrate this holiday, and if the weather is [present simple] good, they have [present simple] picnics or barbecues in order to enjoy the outdoors. I guess people really love [present simple] eating outside, especially if they have to be [present simple + infinitive] inside during the week at an office job. In my family, for instance, we go out [present simple – phrasal verb] to my grandfather's cottage in the countryside the night before. Then, the next morning we get up [present simple – phrasal verb] and set [present simple] a table outside and get [present simple] some food ready. We spend [present simple] the day chatting with each other, and my grandma makes [present simple] a cake as a special treat that we eat [present simple] later in the day. We have celebrated [present perfect] the holiday like this for as long as I can remember. Actually, I am really looking forward to [present continuous – phrasal verb] celebrating the day with my family again when I return [present simple] to my country at the end of this course.

MODEL ANSWER TEST 2 – TASK 3

Examiner: We have been talking about national festivals and celebrations in your country. I'd like to continue talking about this topic in part 3 of the test. Could you describe the importance of national festivals?

Student: I think that observing and celebrating national festivals is important because people need to have a day off to relax once in a while. If people never had a day off work, they would get really fed up, so celebrations help people to avoid getting burnt out.

Examiner: What are some of the effects of international festivals and events, like the Olympics, for example?

Student: Events like the Olympics are extremely important because they bring different cultures together. When people from different cultures interact with each other, they become more understanding and tolerant of one another. Hopefully, as global events and celebrations become more popular, there will be fewer cultural stereotypes and misconceptions.

Examiner: Can you discuss how international festivals have changed over time?

Student: Compared to events in the past, events nowadays seem to have a much more international flavour. There is a much higher level of cultural diversity because more participants from more countries are taking part than in the past. It could even be the case that, if certain countries hadn't been so culturally insular in the past, perhaps we wouldn't have witnessed certain terrorist incidents in recent years.

Examiner: Can you analyse the extent to which international festivals influence the future of a host country?

Student: Well, there seem to be two views. Some people hold the view that hosting an international event is extremely costly and places a future financial burden on the host country. On the other hand, other people seem to think exactly the opposite: that hosting an international event brings more attention to a country and that the tourist economy of the country will expand in the future as more people will come to the host country on holiday.

Examiner: Could you speculate about how festivals might change in the future?

Student: If possible, I'd like to see festivals become even more international than they are now. The way I see it, richer countries could help to finance participation by citizens from poorer countries.

Examiner: Thank you. That is the end of the test.

COMMENTS ON MODEL ANSWER TEST 2 – TASK 3

Comments: The conditional sentences that the student uses have been underlined in the dialogue below. The type of conditional is provided in brackets after each sentence. Also notice the useful phrases, provided in **bold**.

Examiner: We have been talking about national festivals and celebrations in your country. I'd like to continue talking about this topic in part 3 of the test. Could you describe the importance of national festivals?

Student: I think that observing and celebrating national festivals is important because people need to have a day off to relax once in a while. If people never *had* a day off work, they *would get* really fed up [second conditional], so celebrations help people to avoid getting burnt out.

Examiner: What are some of the effects of international festivals and events, like the Olympics, for example?

Student: Events like the Olympics are extremely important because they bring different cultures together. When people from different cultures *interact* with each other, they *become* more understanding and tolerant of one another [zero conditional]. **Hopefully**, as global events and celebrations become more popular, there will be fewer cultural stereotypes and misconceptions.

Examiner: Can you discuss how international festivals have changed over time?

Student: Compared to events in the past, events nowadays seem to have a much more international flavour. There is a much higher level of cultural diversity because more participants from more countries are taking part than in the past. **It could even be the case that,** <u>if certain countries *hadn't been* so culturally insular in the past, perhaps we *wouldn't have witnessed* certain terrorist incidents in recent years</u> [third conditional].

Examiner: Can you analyse the extent to which international festivals influence the future of a host country?

Student: Well, there seem to be two views. **Some people hold the view that** hosting an international event is extremely costly and places a future financial burden on the host country. **On the other hand, other people seem to think** exactly the opposite: that hosting an international event brings more attention to a country and that the tourist economy of the country will expand in the future as more people will come to the host country on holiday.

Examiner: Could you speculate about how festivals might change in the future?

Student: If possible, I'd like to see festivals become even more international than they are now. **The way I see it**, richer countries could help to finance participation by citizens from poorer countries.

Examiner: Thank you. That is the end of the test.

PRACTICE SPEAKING TEST 3 – TASK 1

The examiner asks the candidate familiar questions about him- or herself, work, studies or hobbies.

EXAMPLE

Can you tell me something about:

- your life in this city
- your day-to-day routine
- what you like about your daily routine
- what you dislike about your daily routine

PRACTICE SPEAKING TEST 3 – TASK 2

The examiner will give you some information on a topic. You will have two minutes to talk about the topic. You will have one minute beforehand to prepare for your talk. You can make notes to help you prepare if you so wish.

> I would like you to describe a house or flat in which you have recently lived.
>
> Talk about:
>
> - What kind of accommodation it was.
>
> - Why you liked or disliked it.
>
> - What drawbacks the accommodation had.

PRACTICE SPEAKING TEST 3 – TASK 3

Discussion topics:

The importance of housing

Example questions:

Describe the importance of adequate housing in your country.

Compare the differences between housing in your country with housing in another country.

Evaluate the effects of the shortage of adequate housing on a population.

Housing and society

Example questions:

Discuss how the housing needs of a population have changed over time.

Analyse the extent to which housing problems might lead to other social problems.

Speculate about how housing might change in the future.

MODEL ANSWER TEST 3 – TASK 1

Examiner: In the first part of the test, I'm going to ask you some questions about yourself. Could you please tell me about your life in this city?

Student: Yes, I live in the older part of the city, in a house that has been converted into flats. I have really liked living there so far because it is close to the shops and the sport centre, although I have to take the bus to come to class.

Examiner: What is your day-to-day routine?

Student: I come to the university every day at 9:00 in the morning for English classes. I have class until 4:00 in the afternoon, and then I usually study in the library for a couple of hours after that, so I am here most days until about 6:00. I pack a lunch with something like a sandwich and some crisps the night before so that I have something to eat in the day. Getting food from the vending machines can be so expensive, and the food sometimes isn't very fresh.

Examiner: What do you like about your daily routine?

Student: I really enjoy studying English, and my teachers have been so helpful to me. I also really like my time in the library because, even though I am studying, I work at my own pace, so it feels more like free time to me.

Examiner: What do you dislike about your daily routine?

Student: Well, I don't like taking the bus very much. I'm not saying that I detest it exactly, but it's not very nice some days, especially when there has been an accident or if the bus is crowded.

COMMENTS ON MODEL ANSWER TEST 3 – TASK 1

Comments: The verbs that the student uses have been underlined in the dialogue. The verb tense is provided in brackets after each verb.

Examiner: In the first part of the test, I'm going to ask you some questions about yourself. Could you please tell me about your life in this city?

Student: Yes, I live [present simple] in the older part of the city, in a house that has been converted [present perfect – passive] into flats. I have really liked [present perfect] living there so far because it is [present simple] close to the shops and the sport centre, although I have to take [present simple + infinitive] the bus to come to class.

Examiner: What is your day-to-day routine?

Student: I come [present simple] to the university every day at 9:00 in the morning for English classes. I have [present simple] class until 4:00 in the afternoon, and then I usually study [present simple] in the library for a couple of hours after that, so I am [present simple] here most days until about 6:00. I pack [present simple] a lunch with something like a sandwich and some crisps the night before so that I have [present simple] something to eat in the day. Getting food from the vending machines can be [modal verb] so expensive, and the food sometimes isn't [present simple] very fresh.

Examiner: What do you like about your daily routine?

Student: I really enjoy [present simple] studying English, and my teachers have been [present perfect] so helpful to me. I also really like [present simple] my time in the library because, even though I am studying [present continuous], I work [present simple] at my own pace, so it feels [present simple] more like free time to me.

Examiner: What do you dislike about your daily routine?

Student: Well, I don't like [present simple] taking the bus very much. I'm not saying [present continuous] that I detest [present simple] it exactly, but it's not very nice some days, especially when there has been [present perfect] an accident or if the bus is [present simple] crowded.

MODEL ANSWER TEST 3 – TASK 2

Here is the prompt card again for your reference:

> I would like you to describe a house or flat in which you have recently lived.
>
> Talk about:
>
> - What kind of accommodation it was.
>
> - Why you liked or disliked it.
>
> - What drawbacks the accommodation had.

Student: Before coming here to take this course, I lived in a large house with my family. The house has been in the family for five generations. I mean, my great-great-grandfather built the house one hundred and fifty years ago, and my family has lived in it ever since then. It is a detached house just outside the outskirts of the city, so we have been able to live there in relative peace and quiet beyond the hustle and bustle of city life. The house consists of two living rooms, six bedrooms, three bathrooms and a large kitchen. I really like the house because, of course, I have a lot of happy memories about growing up in this place. But I also like it just as a house because it is so spacious. Having two living rooms is really nice too because my siblings and I can go to different rooms to watch different programmes on TV, for example. I was also able to have my own bedroom when I was a child, which I really liked. Well . . . I think that having to share a bedroom with my sister would have been difficult because she and I are very different people. The house does have a couple of drawbacks, though. Like any older house, it has a few problems with maintenance. For instance, the hot water system breaks down sometimes or the roof leaks, so my father is always busy organising repairs to the house. Another issue is the fact that the house is outside the city, as I said before. My father has to commute into the city centre every day for work, and that makes him a bit tired. Besides that, sometimes it's a bit of a hassle for my friends to come visit me because they have to take the train to come to my house. So, from that perspective, perhaps a house in the suburbs would be more convenient.

COMMENTS ON MODEL ANSWER TEST 3 – TASK 2

Comments: The verbs that the student uses have been underlined in the dialogue. The verb tense is provided in brackets after each verb.

Student: Before coming here to take this course, I lived [past simple] in a large house with my family. The house has been [present perfect] in the family for five generations. I mean, my great-great-grandfather built [past simple] the house one hundred and fifty years ago, and my family has lived [present perfect] in it ever since then. It is [present simple] a detached house just outside the outskirts of the city, so we have been [present perfect] able to live there in relative peace and quiet beyond the hustle and bustle of city life. The house consists [present simple] of two living rooms, six bedrooms, three bathrooms, and a large kitchen. I really like [present simple] the house because, of course, I have [present simple] a lot of happy memories about growing up in this place. But I also like [present simple] it just as a house because it is [present simple] so spacious. Having two living rooms is [present simple] really nice too because my siblings and I can go [modal verb + base form] to different rooms to watch different programmes on TV, for example. I was [past simple] also able to have my own bedroom when I was [past simple] a child, which I really liked [past simple]. Well . . . I think that having to share a bedroom with my sister would have been [modal verb + present perfect] difficult because she and I are [present simple] very different people. The house does have [present emphatic form] a couple of drawbacks, though. Like any older house, it has [present simple] a few problems with maintenance. For instance, the hot water system breaks down [present simple – phrasal verb] sometimes or the roof leaks [present simple], so my father is [present simple] always busy organising repairs to the house. Another issue is the fact that the house is [present simple] outside the city, as I said before. My father has to commute [present simple + infinitive] into the city centre every day for work, and that makes [present simple] him a bit tired. Besides that, sometimes it's a bit of a hassle for my friends to come visit me because they have to take [present simple + infinitive] the train to come to my house. So, from that perspective, perhaps a house in the suburbs would be [modal verb] more convenient.

MODEL ANSWER TEST 3 – TASK 3

Examiner: We have been talking about houses and apartments in the second part of the test. Now I am going to ask you a few more questions about this topic. Can you describe the importance of adequate housing in your country?

Student: Adequate housing is really a significant social issue in my country. The problem is that there isn't adequate social housing, and this forces some people to live in slums or shanty towns. So, I would say that this is one of the most pressing social problems in my country.

Examiner: What are the effects of the shortage of adequate housing on a population?

Student: In my country, it seems like the housing shortage has a link to crime. In other words, it appears that when citizens don't get enough support from the government in the form of housing benefit and other types of welfare payments, then some people will turn to crime in order to have enough money to live. Some people have the view that if the government really cared about people, it would support them in the form of greater financial assistance.

Examiner: Can you compare the differences between housing in your country with housing in another country?

Student: The difference has to do with governmental policy. The housing shortage in my country has caused some people to feel disillusioned with the government's policy. Some people believe that if the government had been interested in solving the problem, it would have done something about it years ago. This is a big contrast to countries like the UK, where there has been a robust social housing programme for a number of decades.

Examiner: To what extent do housing problems lead to other social problems?

Student: As I was saying, crime is probably the most noticeable social problem. But, I think other problems like drug abuse can also be present in the society, because people may turn to drugs and other substances as a way to escape their problems.

Examiner: Can you speculate about how housing might change in the future?

Student: Based on the failure of the government of my country to act on this issue in the past, I think that, unfortunately, there won't be much change in the future. Well . . . it might be that crime will continue to increase to such a serious level that the government will finally decide to review its policies.

Examiner: Thank you. That's the end of the speaking exam.

COMMENTS ON MODEL ANSWER TEST 3 – TASK 3

Comments: The conditional sentences that the student uses have been underlined in the dialogue below. The type of conditional is provided in brackets after each sentence. Finally, you should study the useful phrases, provided in **bold**.

Examiner: We have been talking about houses and apartments in the second part of the test. Now I am going to ask you a few more questions about this topic. Can you describe the importance of adequate housing in your country?

Student: Adequate housing is really a significant social issue in my country. **The problem is that** there isn't adequate social housing, and this forces some people to live in slums or shanty towns. So, **I would say that** this is one of the most pressing social problems in my country.

Examiner: What are the effects of the shortage of adequate housing on a population?

Student: In my country, **it seems like** the housing shortage has a link to crime. **In other words**, **it appears that** <u>when citizens *don't get* enough support from the government in the form of housing benefit and other types of welfare payments, then some people *will turn* to crime in order to have enough money to live</u> [first conditional]. **Some people have the**

view that <u>if the government really *cared* about people, it *would support* them in the form of greater financial assistance.</u> [second conditional]

Examiner: Can you compare the differences between housing in your country with housing in another country?

Student: The difference has to do with governmental policy. The housing shortage in my country has caused some people to feel disillusioned with the government's policy. **Some people believe that** <u>if the government *had been* interested in solving the problem, it *would have done* something about it years ago.</u> [third conditional] **This is a big contrast to** countries like the UK, where there has been a robust social housing programme for a number of decades.

Examiner: To what extent do housing problems lead to other social problems?

Student: As I was saying, crime is probably the most noticeable social problem. But, **I think** other problems like drug abuse can also be present in the society, because people may turn to drugs and other substances as a way to escape their problems.

Examiner: Can you speculate about how housing might change in the future?

Student: Based on the failure of the government of my country to act on this issue in the past, **I think that**, unfortunately, there won't be much change in the future. Well . . . **it might be that** crime will continue to increase to such a serious level that the government will finally decide to review its policies.

Examiner: Thank you. That's the end of the speaking exam.

PART 8 – 300 Additional Speaking Practice Test Questions

100 Prompt Cards for IELTS Speaking Task 2

Now try these practice speaking tests for IELTS speaking task 2. When you have finished, you can find in the next section the task 3 category that matches the topic of your Task 2 prompt.

Prompt Card 1: (Topic – News, Media and Technology)
I'd like you to describe some good news that you have heard recently. Talk about:
- What the news was
- Why it made you happy
- Any other important information

Prompt Card 2: (Topic – Health)
Talk about a stressful day you had recently. Describe:
- What the stressful event was
- Why it was stressful
- How you reacted to it

Prompt Card 3: (Topic – Free Time, Hobbies and Leisure)
Tell me about a pastime that you enjoy doing. Discuss:
- What the pastime is
- Why you enjoy it
- When and where you do it

Prompt Card 4: (Topic – Education)
Describe a place where you like to study. Talk about:
- Where it is
- What the place looks like
- Why it is good for studying

Prompt Card 5: (Topic – Culture and Cultural Events)
Talk about a thoughtful gift that you have received recently. Describe
- What the gift was
- Who gave it to you
- Why you enjoyed it

Prompt Card 6: (Topic – Memories and Remembering)
I'd like you to tell me about something you celebrated recently. Talk about:
- Who was there
- What happened
- When it happened
- Where you were

Prompt Card 7: (Topic – Travel and Tourism)
I'd like you to describe a recent trip to me. Discuss:
- Where you went
- What you saw
- Whether you enjoyed it
- Whether you want to go again

Prompt Card 8: (Topic – Family and Friends)
Describe a time you went out with friends. Talk about:
- Who was with you
- Where you went
- What you did
- How you felt

Prompt Card 9: (Topic – Animals)
Discuss an experience that you have had with an animal or pet. Tell me about:
- What animal it was
- What happened
- How you felt

Prompt Card 10: (Topic – Shopping and Consumerism)
Talk about a time you went shopping. Discuss:
- Where you were
- What you bought
- Who was with you

Prompt Card 11: (Topic – Jobs and Employment)
I'd like you to describe a job or task that you have had to do. Describe:
- What the job was
- What you did
- Whether you enjoyed it

Prompt Card 12: (Topic – Role Models)
Describe a person who has had a major influence on your life. Tell me about:
- Who the person was
- How the person influenced you
- Why you listened to the person

Prompt Card 13: (Topic – Education)
Talk about your favourite academic subject. Please discuss:
- What the subject is
- Why you enjoy it
- What aspects of it you like the most

Prompt Card 14: (Topic – Culture; News, Media and Technology)
I'd like you to describe something about modern life that you dislike. Describe:
- What is the thing that you dislike
- Where it is
- What it looks like
- Why you dislike it

Prompt Card 15: (Topic – Food and Nutrition)
Discuss a meal that you enjoyed. Please tell me about:
- What the food was
- Where you were
- Who served you the food
- Who was with you

Prompt Card 16: (Topic – Health)
I'd like you to tell me how you try to stay healthy. Describe:
- What you do
- How it makes you feel
- Why you think it is healthy

Prompt Card 17: (Topic – Music and Entertainment)
Describe the kind of music or songs that you enjoy. Discuss:
- What kind of music it is
- Where you like to listen to it
- Why you enjoy it

Prompt Card 18: (Topic – Health)
Talk about a time when you felt nervous. Please describe:
- Where you were
- What you were doing
- What you did to try to feel calm

Prompt Card 19: (Topic – Education)
I'd like you to describe something that you learned when you were younger. Please tell me about:
- What you learned
- Why you remember it
- Why you think it is important

Prompt Card 20: (Topic – Making Plans)
Discuss your goals or ambitions. Please mention:
- What your goals are
- Why you have these ambitions
- What you hope to achieve

Prompt Card 21: (Topic – Music and Entertainment; Education)
I'd like you to tell me about a particular skill or talent you have. Describe:
- What the skill or talent is
- How you learned it
- Why it is useful

Prompt Card 22: (Topic – Free Time, Hobbies and Leisure)
Describe the time of day you like the best. Please tell me about:
- What time of day it is
- Why you enjoy it
- How it makes you feel

Prompt Card 23: (Topic – Transport; Travel; Family and Friends)
Talk about a time when you had to wake up much earlier than usual. Discuss:
- Why you had to get up early
- Where you were going
- How you felt

Prompt Card 24: (Topic – Towns and Cities)
I'd like you to tell me about some place in the world that is changing. Please describe:
- Where the place it
- How it is changing
- If the change is good or bad

Prompt Card 25: (Topic – Culture and Cultural Events)
Discuss an important event in your life. Please tell me about:
- What the event was
- Where you were
- Why it was important

Prompt Card 26: (Topic – Social Media)
I'd like you to describe something you like to do online. Describe:
- What the activity is
- Where you are on online
- Why you enjoy it

Prompt Card 27: (Topic – Children)
Describe a memorable event from your childhood. Tell me about:
- What the event was
- Why it was memorable
- How you felt about it

Prompt Card 28: (Topic – Making Plans)
Talk about a time when you had to change your plans. Discuss:
- What your plans were
- Why you had to change them
- What the new plan was

Prompt Card 29: (Topic – Towns and Cities)
I'd like you to describe a place where you would like to live. Describe:
- Where the place is
- What it looks like
- Why you like it

Prompt Card 30: (Topics – New, Media and Technology; Music and Entertainment)
Discuss a famous person that you admire. Tell me about:
- Who the person is
- Why the person is famous
- Why you admire the person

Prompt Card 31: (Topics – Culture; Travel; Free Time)
I'd like you to tell me about the last time you felt really excited about something. Please mention:
- What the situation was
- What you were doing
- Why you were excited

Prompt Card 32: (Topic – Transport)
Describe a journey you made in a car. Describe:
- Where you were going
- Why you were going there
- Whether you enjoyed it

Prompt Card 33: (Topic – Education)
Talk about a school you have attended. Please discuss:
- Where the school was
- What the school was like
- Whether you liked it or not

Prompt Card 34: (Topic – Family and Friends)
I'd like tell me about the most intelligent person you know. Please tell me about:
- Who the person is
- What skills the person has
- Whether you admire the person

Prompt Card 35: (Topic – Shopping and Consumerism; Culture and Cultural Events)
Discuss an advertisement that you have seen recently. Please describe:
- Where the advertisement was
- What was being advertised
- What your opinion was of the advertisement

Prompt Card 36: (Topic – Family and Friends)
I'd like you to tell me about a person with whom you enjoy spending time. Tell me about:
- Who the person is
- What you usually do with the person
- Why you enjoy it

Prompt Card 37: (Topic – Arts and Crafts)
Describe a handmade item or product that is made in your home country. Discuss:
- What the item is
- Where it is made
- How it is made

Prompt Card 38: (Topic – Television)
Talk about a time when you were really bored by something on television. Please tell me about:
- Where you were
- What was happening
- Why you were bored

Prompt Card 39: (Topic – Communication)
I'd like tell me about a difficult situation you have had when trying to speak English. Please mention:
- Where you were
- What the situation was
- How you felt

Prompt Card 40: (Topic – Food and Nutrition)
Discuss a barbeque or picnic that you attended. Describe:
- Where you were
- How the weather was
- Who you were with

Prompt Card 41: (Topic – Education)
I'd like you to tell me about your favourite teacher. Please tell me about:
- Who the teacher was
- What the teacher taught you
- Why the teacher was your favourite

Prompt Card 42: (Topic – Family and Friends)
Describe a time when you met someone by chance. Discuss:
- Where you were
- How you met
- What you talked about

Prompt Card 43: (Topic – Environment)
Talk about a place where there is a lot of pollution. Describe:
- Where it is
- What has caused the pollution
- What people think about the situation

Prompt Card 44: (Topic – Memories and Remembering)
I'd like you to talk about a time when you lost something or thought you had lost something. Tell me about:
- What you lost
- How you felt
- Whether you found the item again

Prompt Card 45: (Topic – Making Decisions)
Discuss a decision you made recently that you regret. Please mention:
- What the decision was
- Why you made the decision
- Why you regretted the decision

Prompt Card 46: (Topic – Relationships)
I'd like you to describe an ideal marriage or relationship. Please describe:
- The characteristics of the people
- How the people act towards each other
- Why the relationship is an ideal one

Prompt Card 47: (Topic – Making plans)
Describe a personal achievement that you have accomplished. Tell me about:
- What the achievement was
- How you planned to achieve it
- How you felt about it

Prompt Card 48: (Topic – Environment)
Talk about your favourite season of the year. Please mention:
- What the season is
- How the weather is
- Why it is your favourite

Prompt Card 49: (Topic – Travel and Tourism)
I'd like you to describe a place that tourists visit in your home country. Discuss:
- What the place is
- Where the place is
- Why tourists come to see it

Prompt Card 50: (Topic – Movies)
Discuss your favourite movie star. Tell me about:
- Who the person is
- What movies they have been in
- Why the person is your favourite

Prompt Card 51: (Topic – Music and Entertainment)
I'd like you to describe your favourite singer. Discuss:
- Who the singer is
- What kind of songs the person sings
- Why the singer is your favourite

Prompt Card 52: (Topic – Towns and Cities)
Talk about a town or city where you have lived. Please mention:
- Where the town or city was
- What was interesting about the place
- Whether you enjoyed it

Prompt Card 53: (Topic – Family and Friends)
Tell me about a new friend that you have make recently. Describe:
- Who it was
- How you met
- Why you became friends

Prompt Card 54: (Topic – Arts and Crafts)
Describe a place where there are a lot of decorations. Please tell me about:
- Where it was
- What the decorations looked like
- Whether you liked it or not

Prompt Card 55: (Topic – Family and Friends)
Talk about a person who is very friendly. Describe:
- Who the person is
- How you came to know the person
- How they act with other people

Prompt Card 56: (Topic – Public Places)
I'd like you to tell me about a place that is very lively. Please mention:
- Where the place is
- Why it is lively
- Why people enjoy going there

Prompt Card 57: (Topic – Clothing)
I'd like you to describe a person who wears unusual clothes. Discuss:
- What kind of clothes the person wears
- Why the clothes are unusual
- Whether you like the clothes or not

Prompt Card 58: (Topic – News, Media and Technology)
Describe a time when your computer broke down. Tell me about:
- When it was
- What happened
- What you did about it

Prompt Card 59: (Topic – Memories and Remembering)
Discuss a time when you had to memorise something. Please describe:
- What you had to memorise
- Why you had to memorise it
- How you did it

Prompt Card 60: (Topic – Children)
Talk about a game that you enjoyed playing during your childhood. Tell me:
- What the game was
- How the game was played
- Why you enjoyed it

Prompt Card 61: (Topic – News, Media and Technology)
I'd like you to describe a famous person who is often in the news. Please mention:
- Who the person is
- Why the person is famous
- Why the person in the news

Prompt Card 62: (Topic – Towns and Cities)
Describe a part of a city or town that you like spending time in. Discuss:
- Where the town or city is
- What the town or city looks like
- Why you like it

Prompt Card 63: (Topic – Environment)
Talk about the kind of weather that you enjoy the most. Please describe:
- What kind of weather it is
- Why you enjoy it
- What you like to do during it

Prompt Card 64: (Topic – Towns and Cities)
I'd like you to describe something about your hometown that you dislike. Please tell me about:
- Where it is
- How it looks
- Why you dislike it

Prompt Card 65: (Topic – Family and Friends)
Describe the last time when you saw a group of people smiling. Please mention:
- What the occasion was
- Who was there
- Why they were smiling

Prompt Card 66: (Topic – Education)
I'd like you to tell me how you study for exams. Discuss:
- What kind of exams you have
- How you study for them
- Why you study this way

Prompt Card 67: (Topic – Free Time, Hobbies and Leisure)
Describe the kind of party that you most enjoy. Please mention:
- What happens at the party
- Who is there
- Why you enjoy it

Prompt Card 68: (Topic – Communication, Jobs and Employment)
Talk about a time when you had to work with others in a group. Please tell me about:
- Who was in the group
- What kind of work you had to do
- Whether it was a good experience or not

Prompt Card 69: (Topic – Towns and Cities)
I'd like you to describe a tall building in your city or a city near you. Please mention:
- Where the building is
- Why it was built
- Whether you like it or not

Prompt Card 70: (Topic – Role Models)
Please talk about a creative person that you admire. Discuss:
- Who the person is
- What skills the person has
- Why you admire the person

Prompt Card 71: (Topic – Culture and Cultural Events)
I'd like you to tell me about a tradition in your home country. Please describe:
- What the tradition is
- What happens when the tradition takes place
- Whether you enjoy it

Prompt Card 72: (Topic – Humour; Social Media)
Describe something funny that you have seen on social media. Please discuss:
- What the social media platform was
- What the situation was
- Why it was funny

Prompt Card 73: (Topic – Food and Nutrition)
Talk about a time when you were served some food that you didn't enjoy. Tell me about:
- Where you were
- Who served the food
- What you did when the food was served

Prompt Card 74: (Topic – Towns and Cities)
I'd like you to tell me about a neighbour that you have had. Please mention:
- Who the person was
- Where the person lived
- What characteristics the person had

Prompt Card 75: (Topic – Memory and Remembering)
Please talk about an occasion when you forgot to do something important. Discuss:
- What the occasion was
- What you forgot to do
- What happened

Prompt Card 76: (Topic – Music and Entertainment)
I'd like you to describe some words that you remember from a song. Tell me:
- What the song is
- What the words are
- Why you remember them

Prompt Card 77: (Topic – Family and Friends)
Describe an event that takes place in your family once a year. Describe:
- What the event is
- When the event happens
- Why your family celebrates this event

Prompt Card 78: (Topic – Telephones)
Talk about an activity that you do on your phone that you enjoy. Discuss:
- What the activity is
- When you do it
- Why you like it

Prompt Card 79: (Topic – Travel; Memories and Remembering)
I'd like you to describe a time when you lost your way. Please mention:
- When it happened
- Where you were
- Why you got lost

Prompt Card 80: (Topic – Family and Friends)
Please tell me about a photograph that you like a lot. Please talk about:
- What is in the photograph
- Where the photograph is
- Why you like it

Prompt Card 81: (Topic – Giving Advice)
I'd like you to tell me about a time when you gave some advice to a friend. Discuss:
- Why the friend needed advice
- What the advice was
- Whether your friend followed your advice

Prompt Card 82: (Topic – Disagreements)
Describe a disagreement that took place between two of your friends. Please mention:
- What the disagreement was
- Why they disagreed
- Whether they resolved the disagreement

Prompt Card 83: (Topic – Communication)
Talk about the first time you had to speak to someone in a foreign language. Describe:
- Where you were
- What you talked about
- Whether the experience was good or not

Prompt Card 84: (Topic – Helping Others)
I'd like tell me about a time when you helped someone else. Discuss:
- Who the person was
- Why the person needed help
- What you did to help the person

Prompt Card 85: (Topic – Working Abroad)
Describe a job that you would like to have in a foreign country. Tell me:
- What the job is
- Where it is
- Why you would like it

Prompt Card 86: (Topic – Travel and Tourism; Family and Friends)
I'd like you to tell me about a hotel or special place where you have stayed. Describe:
- Where it is
- What it looks like
- Whether you enjoy staying there

Prompt Card 87: (Topic – Children)
Describe an item or toy that was your favourite thing during your childhood. Tell me about:
- What the item or toy looked like
- Who gave it to you
- Why it was your favourite

Prompt Card 88: (Topic – Arts and Crafts)
Talk about a time when you have seen a piece of art. Describe:
- Where it was
- What it looked like
- Whether you liked it or not

Prompt Card 89: (Topic – Giving Advice)
I'd like tell me about a person who has given you some advice. Please discuss:
- Who the person is
- What advice the person gave
- Whether you followed the advice

Prompt Card 90: (Topic – Food and Nutrition)
Tell me about a time when you ate something unusual for the first time. Please mention:
- What the food was
- Where you were
- Whether you enjoyed it

Prompt Card 91: (Topic – Making Promises)
I'd like you to tell me about a time that you made a promise to someone. Describe:
- What you promised
- Why you promised it
- Whether you kept your promise

Prompt Card 92: (Topic – Family and Friends; Communication)
Describe a time when you had contact with a friend who you hadn't seen in a long time. Tell me about:
- Who the friend was
- How long you had lost contact with the friend
- What happened when you made contact again

Prompt Card 93: (Topic – Disagreements)
Talk about a time when you had a disagreement with someone. Discuss:
- What the situation was
- Why you disagreed
- Whether you resolved the disagreement

Prompt Card 94: (Topic – Free Time, Hobbies and Leisure)
I'd like you to talk about a time when you attended a sporting event. Please mention:
- What sport it was
- Why you attended it
- Whether you enjoyed it

Prompt Card 95: (Topic – News, Media and Technology)
Discuss an item that has been in the international news recently. Please talk about:
- What the news is
- Why it is in the news
- What opinions people have about it

Prompt Card 96: (Topic – Shopping and Consumerism)
I'd like you to describe an item that you bought recently that made you feel satisfied. Discuss:
- What the item was
- Why you bought it
- Why you were satisfied

Prompt Card 97: (Topic – Transport)
Describe a trip that you have to take often but that you don't enjoy. Tell me about:
- Where you go
- Why you have to go there
- Why you don't enjoy it

Prompt Card 98: (Topic – Making Decisions)
Talk about a time when you changed your mind about something or someone. Describe:
- What your original opinion was
- What your opinion is now
- Why you changed your mind

Prompt Card 99: (Topic – Communication)
I'd like you to describe a conversation that made you feel bored. Tell me about:
- What was being discussed
- Who was there
- Why you were bored

Prompt Card 100: (Topic – Public Places; Children)
Please tell me about a time when you saw children misbehaving in a public place. Discuss:
- Where it was
- Who was there
- What was happening

200 Speaking Practice Test Questions for Task 3

Now try these practice speaking tests for IELTS speaking task 3.

Animals

101) The death of an animal can be just as difficult as the death of a loved one. Do you agree?

102) Should the government do more in order to protect animal welfare?

103) What are the advantages and disadvantages of a vegetarian diet?

104) Can you speculate how our relationship with animals might change in the future?

Arts and Crafts

105) Are arts and hand-made crafts more important now that in the past?

106) Why are arts and crafts important for society and culture?

107) What can be done to draw more attention to arts and crafts?

108) Should art be a compulsory subject in schools?

109) Should the government give more money to support arts and crafts?

Children

110) How should parents treat their children?

111) How should children behave towards their parents?

112) Do you think that adult children should still obey their parents?

113) What are the reasons why a person or a couple would prefer not to have children?

114) Should the government pay the parents of young children so that one of the parents can stay at home to look after the children?

Clothing

115) How have clothing styles changed in recent years?

116) In what way will clothing change in the future?

117) Can you speculate why people like to wear unusual clothes?

118) Should we be more mindful about people who work in clothing factories in poor conditions?

119) People should buy less clothing in order to project the environment from the damage caused by the manufacture of clothes. Do you agree?

Communication

120) How have communication styles changed compared to the past?

121) What can be done to improve communication in the workplace?

122) Digital technology has made people lazy at communicating. Do you agree?

123) What are the advantages and disadvantages of face-to-face communication compared to digital communication?

124) Do you think communication between people and groups will improve in the future?

125) What are some of the causes of miscommunication and misunderstanding between people?

Culture and Cultural Events

126) Why do different cultures celebrate events such as birthdays differently?

127) What role does advertising play in your culture?

128) What can different cultures learn from each other?

129) What is the importance of festivals and national holidays in your culture?

130) Do you think that special events such as weddings will change in your culture in the future?

Disagreements

131) What causes disagreements to occur between people?

132) What is the best way to resolve a disagreement?

133) Is it a good idea to try to resolve a disagreement between two of your friends?

134) It is better to insist on what you want instead of compromising. Do you agree?

135) Is there ever a positive side to disagreements between people?

Education

136) What is your opinion about the way English is taught in your home country?

137) How are attitudes about education different today than in the past?

138) In your opinion, should a school teach creative subjects like art and dance?

139) How important is it for schools to have computers in their classrooms?

140) To what extent does a person's choice of university affect his or her success later in life?

141) What changes do you think will take place in education in your country in the future?

Environment

142) In what way is pollution affecting the weather and the seasons?

143) Is the environment in danger in your country?

144) Why is it important to protect the environment?

145) How can the problem of pollution be solved?

146) Do you think that pollution will get worse in the future? Why?

Family and Friends

147) Is friendship important in the culture of your country?

148) How have family relationships changed in your country in recent years?

149) What are the causes of conflict within families?

150) What kinds of conflicts can occur between a person's family and a person's friends?

151) Do you think that family relationships are more important than friendships?

152) What can be done to help make family members feel closer to each other?

153) How to you think family relationships will change in the future?

Food and Nutrition

154) Can you compare and contrast the types of food people eat in your country with the food that is eaten in the UK / US / Australia?

155) Are people's eating habits different now than in the past?

156) Do you think that most people in your country eat a heathy diet?

157) Would most people prefer traditional food or fast food?

158) Should children be taught about nutrition in school?

159) What can be done to prevent people in the world from going hungry?

160) Should richer countries help to supply food to poorer countries?

161) How do you think that attitudes about food will change in the future?

Free Time, Hobbies and Leisure

162) What types of leisure activities or sports are the most popular in your country?

163) Why do you think it is important for people to have free time?

164) What are the possible benefits of playing a sport?

165) Why are some hobbies and leisure activities more popular than others?

166) Can you compare leisure activities today with those from the past?

167) To what extent can sporting activities bring people from different cultures closer together?

168) Can you speculate about what types of leisure activities might become more popular in the future?

Giving Advice

169) If someone fails to take your advice, you should stop giving advice in the future. Do you agree?

170) What are the pros and cons of giving advice to friends or family members?

171) In what circumstances should you ignore advice that has been given to you?

172) What consequences can occur when a person fails to follow good advice?

173) Can you speculate about the reasons why people ignore the advice of others?

Helping Others

174) It is better to make others happy before you make yourself happy. Do you agree?

175) Should the government do more to support those from poorer countries?

176) The government should do more to support people in helping professions such as teaching and healthcare. Do you agree?

177) Can society benefit when people help others or does it only help the person who receives support?

178) Should the government do more to help charities?

Health

179) Do you think that stress is one of the major causes of illness in the world today?

180) Is it better for people to have private medical insurance instead of relying on the government for free health care?

181) Most health problems occur because people are not educated about the main causes of poor health. Do you agree?

182) Should richer countries give money to poorer countries to help with their public healthcare?

183) Nowadays many people around the world are extremely overweight. What can be done to solve this problem?

Humour

184) How is humour different now than it was in the past?

185) Some kinds of humour are inappropriate. Do you agree?

186) Do you think humour and comedy will change in the future?

187) What are the reasons why do people need humour in their lives?

188) Can you speculate why something may be humorous to one person but not to another?

Jobs and Employment

189) What are the main causes of unemployment in your country?

190) What can be done to solve the problem of unemployment?

191) What are the main reasons why people feel satisfied with their jobs?

192) Do you think that changing careers in mid-life is a sign of failure?

193) Should teenagers work part-time during their school years? Why or why not?

184) Would you prefer to work for a company or would you rather start your own business?

Making Decisions

195) Impulsive decisions never turn out well. Do you agree?

196) What are the advantages and disadvantages of thinking through something before making a decision?

197) What causes come people to make decisions much more quickly than other people?

198) It is always best to get advice from others before making an important decision. Do you agree?

199) Can you speculate why some people have difficulty making even small decisions?

Making Plans

200) In what situations is it best to follow a plan?

201) It is important to be flexible when making plans. Do you agree?

202) When you fail to plan, you plan to fail. Do you agree?

203) Can you speculate why some people do not like to make plans for anything in their lives?

Making Promises

204) What are the reasons why people make promises to one another?

205) Promises should never be broken. Do you agree?

206) Is it better not to trust someone if they have broken a promise to you in the past?

207) Can you speculate about what would cause a person to break an important promise?

Memories and Remembering

208) Besides mental illness, what causes people to forget something?

209) Special memories are something you carry in your heart. Photographs and mementos are not important. Do you agree?

210) What causes older people to sometimes want to live in the past?

211) Sometimes two people remember the same event very differently. What can cause this to happen?

212) It is important to remember loved ones who have passed away. Do you agree?

Music and Entertainment

213) How have music and other forms of entertainment changed over time?

214) What causes a person to become sentimental about a piece of music?

215) Why are the words to some songs more memorable than others?

216) Famous people should be admired for their creativity, rather than judged on their lifestyles and personal decisions. Do you agree?

217) Highly-paid entertainers should do more to help others. Do you agree?

Movies

218) How have today's movies changed from those in the past?

219) Age restrictions on certain movies should be removed. Do you agree?

220) What are the advantages of going to the cinema instead of watching a movie at home?

221) Most movies nowadays depict too much sex and violence. Do you agree?

222) Can you speculate how movies might change in the future?

News, Media and Technology

223) Can you compare and contrast learning about the news from the radio and from the television?

224) What are the similarities and differences between the news on these two forms of media?

225) What types of publications do people enjoy reading in your country?

226) What sorts of stories are reported on famous people in your country?

227) Are repeated media stories about famous people good or bad for larger society?

228) In what way can films and other media affect the decisions that people make?

229) In your opinion, should people who write for newspapers and blogs be allowed to say whatever they want?

230) In what way can people cause annoyance to others by using technological devices in public?

231) How will the reporting of news in the media change in the future?

232) What can the government do to reduce cyber-crime in the future?

Public places

233) In what way has people's behaviour in public changed when compared to the past?

234) Is it a restriction on people's freedom to ban smoking in public places?

235) Is it appropriate for couples to show affection to each other in public?

236) Should the government do more to keep public places clean?

237) Access to public places should be banned during times of national crisis. Do you agree?

Relationships

238) Do you think dating websites are useful for people looking for a relationship?

239) What is your opinion about people who form romantic relationships with another person at their place of work?

240) Sometimes people have to live far away from each other, but do you think that long-distance relationships can last? Why or why not?

241) What can couples do to feel closer to each other?

242) Should couples live together before they get married to see if they are compatible?

Role Models

243) Who are the most influential people in your country?

244) Who are the best role models: parents, friends, teachers or someone else?

245) Why is it important to have role models?

246) What types of influences and pressures are there on young people in your country?

247) In what way do you think that the educational system in your country influences the lives of young people?

248) What do you think will be the biggest influence on young people in the future?

Social Media

249) Is it a good idea to add a complete stranger to your list of friends on social media?

250) Should everyone take a break from social media from time to time?

251) What are the pros and cons of communicating via social media?

252) Information on social media needs to be read with a sceptical mind. Do you agree?

253) Can you speculate why some people completely object to using social media?

Shopping and Consumerism

254) What are the typical things that a visitor to your country might buy?

255) What types of things do young people in your country like to buy?

256) In your opinion, is it better to spend money or to save money?

257) How have shopping habits in your country changed in recent years?

258) Do possessions bring people true happiness?

259) Can you speculate about the reasons why people enjoy shopping?

260) What can shops do to make shopping more pleasant for the consumer?

261) In your opinion, are most people wise consumers?

262) To what extent does advertising influence people's buying habits?

263) In the future, do you think that most people will do their shopping on the internet?

Telephones

264) In what way are telephone nowadays different than those of the past?

265) What are the pros and cons of smartphones?

266) People should put their phones away when eating with others in a restaurant. Do you agree?

267) Can you speculate why some people do not like to use smartphones?

268) How will telephones and telephone usage change in the future?

Television

269) What types of programmes do young people typically watch in your country?

270) Can you compare and contrast free national television and paid television programmes in your country?

271) In what way can watching television be harmful to children?

272) Should the government ban aggressive and violent TV shows?

273) Can you speculate about the reasons why people like watching television?

Towns and Cities

274) How have towns and cities changed over time?

275) Why do some people prefer living in a big city instead of a small town?

276) What are the advantages and disadvantages of living in a big city?

277) People from larger cities are generally more knowledgeable and sophisticated that people living in the country. Do you agree?

278) Should the government do more to restrict the construction of tall buildings?

Transport

279) How do most people travel long distances in your country?

280) How has transport changed over the past fifty years?

281) What could be done to improve the transport system in your country?

282) Do you think that public transport will become more popular in the future?

283) Should motorcycle driving for those under the age of 25 be banned because it is too dangerous?

284) What could the government of your country do to improve the public transport system?

285) What can be done to encourage people to use public transport instead of private vehicles?

Travel and Tourism

286) What types of things can people learn from travelling?

287) Can you compare and contrast travelling by train and by aeroplane?

288) In what way do tourists disrespect the places that they visit?

289) Can you speculate about the reasons why people enjoy travelling in their free time?

290) In what ways does tourism cause harm to the environment and to local communities?

291) How has tourism changed the way that people live in your country?

292) Does tourism have more advantages or disadvantages for the places that tourists visit?

293) Do you think that the expansion of international tourism will do more harm than good?

294) In what way do you think that tourism will change in your country in the future?

Working abroad

295) Why do some people prefer to work abroad instead of working in their home countries?

296) Working abroad can help to expand a person's mind. Do you agree?

297) Some people need to go abroad to work illegally to try to support their families. What are the dangers of this illegal work?

298) The government should relax immigration rules so that more foreigners can work in your country. Do you agree?

299) Richer countries should do more to invite workers from poorer countries. Do you agree?

300) Native workers should always be given preference over foreign workers. Do you agree?